BEAR GRYLLS GREAT OUTDOOR ADVENTURES

BEAR GRYLLS

Books

To my good friends and family with whom
I have shared so many great adventures
in the past and with whom I hope to share
many more in the future.
This book is for you.

"Life should NOT be a journey to the grave
with the intention of arriving safely in
an attractive and well-preserved body,
but rather to skid in sideways, covered
in scars, body thoroughly used up,
totally worn out and screaming,
"Yahooo – what a ride!""

BEAR GRYLLS
GREAT OUTDOOR ADVENTURES

CONTENTS

OVER THE YEARS I have realized that living a full life isn't about how good we are at things, in fact the world is full of unfulfilled talent; but instead I have seen time and time again that life rewards the persistent.

What counts is developing a cheerfulness and quiet determination to keep going and never give up. That combination of cheerfulness and determination is one of life's secrets to success, yet not many people realize this. We tend to believe it is all about luck and talent. But that's a convenient excuse. The truth is that if you are cheerful and determined, you will inevitably be lucky and succeed. It is a law of the universe. The more you try, the luckier you will get. I'll offer three quick examples.

Firstly, I started learning karate aged thirteen with five friends. They were all better, fitter, stronger and more flexible than me, but after a few months they all quit. I found it hard to motivate myself to get whacked in the mouth every Sunday night during two-hour-long karate classes when I was tucked up cosily at home with a packet of biscuits! But, despite that and the fact that I wasn't that brilliant, I kept going. And in that process of not giving up, I gradually became pretty handy. Years later I got a Second Dan black belt, not because I was talented, but because I was the most persistent. Oh, and my five friends couldn't now defend themselves against a lollipop.

Secondly, when I tried Selection for the SAS, after many months and gallons of sweat, I was failed at the end of one particularly long and arduous march. Part of me thought, 'Sack it, I never want willingly to go through that much pain and discomfort again.' But I also knew that pain, cold and discomfort don't last forever, and that a sense of achievement does. So I tried again; not tentatively, but by throwing my heart and soul into it. And this time I passed. It took two years of my life, with even more blood, sweat and tears than I could ever have imagined. (Sometimes not knowing the hardships ahead is a serious blessing!) It was the hardest and yet most rewarding thing I have ever done. And yes, the pain now is a distant memory and the pride somehow still remains.

For the record: I was never the fittest, never the fastest, but I passed because I was bloody-minded. This is the one quality the SAS look for above skill, leadership or any other character trait – they know the power and value of a determined man.

Finally, there was Everest. I had always heard that around one person in fifty who attempts it actually achieves the summit. But I also knew that statistics are there to be challenged! I climbed for many months on Everest alongside some of the fittest and talented mountaineers in the world and I learnt the hard way that surviving and summiting on Everest is all about being able to motivate yourself when it is truly grim. It is about smiling when it is freezing and keeping going when it is scary. It is about getting up and slogging your guts out, time and time again, day after day. The climbers who don't make it to the top are often those that have been drained of motivation. Day after day of extreme conditions, lonely hours climbing through

What counts is developing a cheerfulness and quiet determination to keep going and never give up.

the cold dawns and the interminable storms bring them down; they slow and eventually give up. But on Everest, as in life, the rewards go to those who can smile, show heart and just keep going. Indeed cheerfulness in adversity is a great trait to develop.

So I will start this book with a great quote:

It is not the critic who counts; not the man who points out how the strong man stumbles, or when the doer of deeds could have done them better. The credit belongs to the man who is actually in the arena, whose face is marred by dust and sweat and blood; who strives valiantly . . . who, at the best, knows, in the end, the triumph of high achievement, and who, at the worst, if he fails, at least fails whilst daring greatly – so that his place shall never be with those cold and timid souls who know neither victory nor defeat . . . For those who have had to fight for it, life has truly a flavour the protected shall never know.

THEODORE ROOSEVELT

So go for it . . . live boldly. Enjoy this book – use it whenever you know deep down that life requires you to get up and live an adventure. And remember, whichever of these chapters you pick to do today, embark on it with good friends or family. Everything in life is more fun when shared – and nothing more so than adventure.

God speed.

Flying and Falling

Adventures in the World's Biggest Playground

ANY BOOK OF Great Adventures would be incomplete without exploring the great and almost infinite realm of the sky. And, man alive, is there a lot of fun to be had above our heads in the world's largest, most dynamic, most exhilarating playground.

I always maintain that the big danger in all aerial sports is summed up in one word: gravity. You can use it, you can exploit it, you can ride it, but you can't beat it. Before you get involved in aerial adventures, remember this: respect gravity, and always cut yourself 10 per cent more margin for error than for any other of the pursuits in this book. If it's working against you, gravity offers very little time to correct mistakes.

But before we look at the dangers, let's briefly look at why flying or falling in the sky can be so liberating and exhilarating, and how you can best exploit the chance to be literally as free as a bird.

As a kid it was agony to have to wait until I was sixteen years old to be allowed to parachute.

From as young as I can remember, the thought of being allowed to hurl myself out of a plane and fly through the air was irresistible. I remember my first ever jump very clearly. I was on a visit to the Royal Marines and had opted to do a static line jump at Dunkeswell in Devon near their headquarters. The instructor who had taken us through the training, gathered us around for one final briefing. He told us if our reserve chutes failed we had one final chance. I was all ears at this point. 'Raise your arms at 90 degrees to your side and then lower them. Now do it again but a bit faster. And again . . . and again . . . faster . . . faster . . .' I was standing there flapping my arms like a crazed chicken still not realizing it was a wind-up. He must have thought I was very wet behind the ears!

But as the smallest member of the group I was somehow picked to leave the aircraft first. During the next 30 minutes if there was an emotion for it, then I felt it. As the plane slowly ascended, I felt first sick, then hollow, then wretched, then dizzy, then faint, then shaky, until eventually, after what seemed like a year, the door opened, the instructor smiled and a big size 10 boot catapulted me out into space. It was truly amazing! I landed like a sack of potatoes and I have never looked back.

As a kid I also loved acrobatics, and I still do. I love doing flick-flacks and back somersaults, but I have learnt that the limiting factor is always that the earth comes up to meet you very fast. The great joy of skydiving is the freedom of being able to do the most free and graceful acrobatics across the sky unhindered.

It takes a bit of practice but the great thing is that it doesn't really matter if your back somersault during a skydive is tidy or not. You are still 3000 metres up in the air, falling at 130mph with the airflow racing around every turn and twist of your body, moulding you into fantastically fun positions. It is about as freeing a sensation as it's possible to experience. You are alone and you are flying, and every move you make with your head or hands and feet has an instant effect on your freefall. It is as pure an art as you can find.

A few years on, there was the small matter of a ripped parachute that had my name on it while jumping in southern Africa that left me with three broken vertebrae and a long stint in military rehabilitation trying to learn to walk properly again. But apart from that eighteen-month hiccup and the odd other scrape, the rest of my time airborne has been a privilege. In my opinion knocks in life are there to give us a chance to show our mettle and to stand up again, stronger and better than ever.

I also got into paragliding, where the freedom is similar to skydiving but slower. This time you are soaring and flying like a bird, gracefully riding airflows and thermals, skimming along mountain ridges. Then, of course, there's paramotoring (taking to the air in a small, powered, one-man paraglider), in which you have even more control. I remember recently on a beautiful, still summer's evening, sitting in my shorts and bare feet watching the sun dipping over the valley. There was low cloud but I could see shafts of sunlight poking through it. So I grabbed my paramotor, strapped it to my back, ran 20 metres through the grass and was airborne.

I climbed up out of the darkening valley and punched through the thin wispy clouds to emerge into blazing sunshine above. For the next hour I followed the contours of the clouds, trailing my feet in the wispy cotton just below me, singing at the top of my voice, all alone above the world. It was heaven. And I truly have no idea why the whole world doesn't do it. There really is so much fun to be had in the sky.

One of the greatest privileges I have had was to paramotor above the height of the summit of Mount Everest in the Himalayas. It was a dream flight, though if truth be told one fraught with

Flying my Royal Navy parachute down to the ground.

Dangerous, but fun! However, you've got to get these sorts of jumps absolutely right.

too many dangers ever to make it worth recommending. The funny thing is, putting the minus 55-degree temperatures and hurricane-force Everest winds aside, the principles of that flight were pretty much the same as for any other one. Watch out for weather, rotor, the ground and water.

> **WARNING**
>
> When it comes to flying or falling, the saying I live by is this: 'There's only one thing worse than being on the ground desperate to be up in the air, and that's being up in the air desperate to be back on the ground.' I have been in far too many bad situations over the years, and it is neither fun nor clever.
>
> And remember this one too – if there is doubt, there is no doubt! It is better to be a little too cautious than a little too gung-ho. And as I once heard: there are old pilots, there are bold pilots, but there are few old and bold pilots! So, trust your instinct, it's the nose of the mind. This is key with aerial activities. It's all about making smart calls and staying alive to fly another day.

Of course, I have learnt a few key things about safety along the way. The first thing to note is that stuff tends to go wrong when you are least experienced (annoyingly!). A lot of my near misses occurred when I was first learning to skydive or paraglide. So always listen carefully to your instructor and be more cautious than you might otherwise be. Check and re-check the weather, be that 10 per cent more cautious than normal and develop a sixth sense of where the dangers will come from. Apart from that: be especially careful in mountains, pull your chute high and practise reserve drills. That's it in a

nutshell. Go get it, guys. The sky is your playground and, sure as eggs is eggs, we only have one life in which to enjoy it.

SKYDIVING

As adrenalin rushes go, nothing beats freefall. If opening the door of a plane at 4000 metres (more than two-and-a-half miles high) and jumping out doesn't give you a buzz, then nothing will. Within six or seven seconds of leaving the plane, you will have reached terminal velocity (around 120mph) and be falling at a rate approaching 60 metres per second. That's more than the height of the Eiffel Tower every five seconds.

You will be in freefall for about a minute, although it can seem much longer. Thinking straight under these conditions can be difficult at first, but after a few more jumps everything from acrobatics to skysurfing and formation flying will become possible.

TRAINING AND EQUIPMENT

The quickest way to learn to skydive is to do an AFF (Accelerated Freefall) course. The course is designed to last a week but, depending on weather conditions, can sometimes be completed within three days. It's designed to be intensive (that's why it's accelerated) and students learn in small groups with the individual attention of two instructors.

The course consists of eight levels with normally one skydive at each level. Level One begins with tuition on the ground and covers both the theory and practice of skydiving. Before the first jump, you'll be taken through every move on terra firma first. You'll know how the equipment works; how to exit the aircraft; how to position the body; the importance of altitude awareness; how to open the parachute and finally how to steer down to the landing area and land safely.

Head down, free flying – one of the hardest disciplines to master.

Ground tuition is followed by a jump from a height of up to 4000 metres accompanied by two instructors who will be freefalling next to you giving in-air coaching via hand-signals and making sure your body position remains stable. On your first few jumps you'll experience about 40–45 seconds of freefall before opening the canopy at 1500 metres.

As you move up the levels learning more skills with each jump, you'll start to jump with only one instructor alongside followed by a solo graduation jump. By the time you're finished, you will have learnt how to turn, move forwards and backwards, loop the loop, how to open the canopy in a stable face-to-earth position, and how to fly it down for a perfect landing. After Level Eight, you'll do ten more consolidation jumps and then you're qualified.

Wingsuit skydiving – as close to being a bird as you'll get.

OLAV ZIPSER AND THE FREEFLY CLOWNS

Creative expression in the air hit new heights in the 1990s when German-born Olav Zipser (aka the 'Father of Freefly') formed a group of freefall acrobats called the Freefly Clowns. The idea was to stretch the boundaries of what was then thought possible when flying through the air and Olav introduced artistic expression into freefall using every possible body position imaginable.

Standing, sitting, falling upside-down or even on your back were all now seen as legitimate freefall techniques. Olav went on to start the first School of Modern Skyflying in his adopted country of Italy and in 1997 started the Space Games dedicated to the 'Art of Human Flight'.

WINGSUITS

Wingsuits have revolutionized the sport of freefall. Designed to help turn the body into an aerofoil just like the wing of a bird or a plane, wingsuits have fabric connecting the arms to the body and between the legs. The overall effect makes the wearer resemble a flying squirrel, hence the nickname 'squirrel suits'.

Wingsuits allow the wearer to glide and mimic the flight of birds more effectively than any other form of flight yet invented. They also increase the time spent in freefall from around a minute to more than three minutes and it's a much quieter experience than the noisy air rush you experience in conventional freefall. Wingsuit formation flying is called – you guessed it – 'flocking', with experienced flyers learning to change direction and speed simultaneously like a flock of birds.

Wingsuits help to turn the body into an aerofoil, just like the wing of a bird or a plane.

Sky surfing requires near-perfect balance.

SKYSURFING

Board sports from surfing, skateboarding and snowboarding are the inspiration behind one of the wildest outdoor sports of them all – skysurfing. Believe me, it's not easy, and it takes a load of practice to become a skilled skysurfer. But, as with all board sports, it's all about balance.

Aerobatics, including loops, spins and rolls, are all possible but the force of the uprushing air on the bottom of the board is so great that it's the easiest thing in the world to flip over into an uncontrolled tumble and that's the last thing you want just when you need to open your canopy!

PARAGLIDING

While fixed-structure enclosed gliding machines have been around since the early days of flight, the technology to fly Harry Potter-like in a flying armchair open to the elements has only been available for the last few decades. And, arguably, only in the last decade or so have these remarkable flying machines been safe enough for anyone to learn to fly without causing themselves a serious injury.

Paragliding over some of the most sublime landscapes on earth, from the Himalayas to the Alps and the Andes, takes some beating

It's hard to resist the urge to fly.

and has restored much of the sense of excitement of aviation's first pioneers. While hang gliders, which have a rigid structure, have been around since the early 1970s, they have now been overtaken in popularity by the paraglider. And for good reason, as the dawn of the age of the paraglider now means that you can carry a flying machine in a rucksack anywhere in the world.

ON A WING AND A PRAYER

In flight a paraglider resembles a magical flying armchair suspended from a spider's web of gossamer cords. The canopy is shaped like a wing with an upper and lower layer of ripstop materials. The two layers are joined at the back with open cells at the front so that on being pulled into the wind the structure inflates to form a solid wing. The inflated canopy then creates lift in much the same way as the wing of an aircraft.

Paragliders can be launched from anywhere high up, a hillside or a mountain, as long as it's clear of obstructions. The only necessity is that the wind is blowing onto the hill and is no stronger than about 15mph. There are paragliding schools all over Europe and the US where you can learn at sites where it is both legal and safe to fly.

You may think there is little difference between a parachute and a paraglider, but there is one important difference: because of its wing-like aerodynamics when inflated, a paraglider can go up as well as down. This is achieved by flying into areas of rising air, of which there are two main types: 'ridge lift' and 'thermals'. The former is caused from the upward draught of a breeze blowing against a hillside, while the latter can potentially be found anywhere and is produced by the sun heating up some pockets of ground

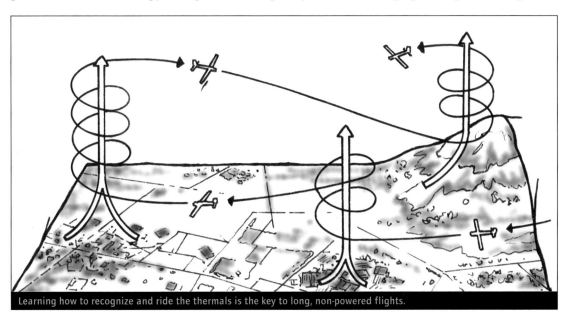

Learning how to recognize and ride the thermals is the key to long, non-powered flights.

One of the scariest moments in my life – taking off for our flight above Everest.

faster than others – fields of ploughed earth, buildings or rock faces for example. This process in turn heats the air above until bubbles of heated air break off and start rising. These are known as thermals.

Rising air is invisible so pilots have to learn to spot the signs (birds circling or the wisps of an embryonic cumulus cloud, for example) and fly towards them. Once mastery of these techniques has been achieved, a paraglider can 'hop' from thermal to thermal for distances that can reach up to several hundred miles.

PARAMOTORING

Paramotors, like the one in which I flew to above Mount Everest, allow far greater flexibility for launching and flying than conventional paragliders. They consist of a propeller and an engine strapped to the back of a pilot's harness surrounded by a protective cage.

Their great advantage is that they can be launched from flat land (like a plain, ordinary field) and will keep the pilot in the air when there is no other available lift.

PARAMOTORING OVER EVEREST

The newest paramotors are electric. They have quieter, more efficient and economical engines, which are better for the environment. The great joy is that they are silent when at idle. You can use the engine to pop back into the thermals, then you can go silent again. This offers the perfect combination of paragliding and paramotoring.

It's a far cry from the expedition I led to fly paramotors to above the height of Everest in 2007. We had the loudest, most powerful machines ever made. The battle we faced was not only the sub zero (minus 60°) temperatures and jet-stream winds, but being able to design a machine that could even reach those extreme Himalayan heights in the first place. The world record was 20,017 feet beforehand. We were aiming to reach 29,000 feet, which was effectively like trying to knock five seconds off the 100 metres sprint.

The normal 20hp engine was replaced by a 100hp one, which was then fuel injected, supercharged, had the exhaust and starter motor removed to save weight and involved us carrying supplementary bottled oxygen and over 30 litres of fuel. No wonder so many people said we would never do it! But we did it, and despite our altimeters freezing at 25,005 feet robbing us of the chance to claim any official records, my machine eventually lifted me above Everest allowing me to film looking over and beyond the summit. It was a flight of dreams and in the process we raised over $2.7 million for children's charities worldwide.

Up into ever-thinner air through the Himalayan giants.

BUNGEE JUMPING

Few activities provoke such an intense reaction in the human brain as falling through the air at terminal velocity. And the closer you are to the ground, the greater the rush. Until recently this usually meant one thing and one thing only: a one-way ticket to the afterlife. But during the 1980s the hitherto suicidal proposition of jumping off a bridge or tall building was turned into a new extreme sport . . . and all without the inconvenience of actually having to die.

Strangely enough, it all started with a documentary by Sir David Attenborough. Early in his career, Sir David made a film about a bizarre initiation ritual still practised by the natives of Pentecost Island in the South Pacific. This involved young initiates throwing themselves off wooden towers with vines round their ankles

to celebrate a successful yam harvest. Normally (though not always), the vines broke their fall before the ground broke their heads.

Inspired by this, two Kiwis – A. J. Hackett and Henry van Asch – developed an elasticated rope made of hundreds of strands of latex to replace the dodgy vines used by the islanders. They called this a 'bungee' and tested their new invention by making a series of extreme jumps from a gondola in the ski resort of Tignes, France. Once they had perfected the equipment, 'AJ' jumped from the arch of the Eiffel Tower in Paris and into the international spotlight. The bungee legend had been born.

The world's first commercial jump site opened on the banks of the Kawarau River near Queenstown, New Zealand in 1988, a site now recognized as the spiritual home of the sport. Since then bungee jumping has spread all over the world with commercially run jumps taking place from bridges, cranes, cable cars, hot air balloons and helicopters, with everything from bikes, sofas and surfboards used as props. Not to mention the exhibitionist's perfect day out: the nude bungee jump.

BASE JUMPING

It's mad, it's bad, and it's very dangerous. But there are still people out there who are willing to risk everything for the biggest thrill of them all. If you get a kick out of bungee jumping, then try to imagine it without the bungee rope attached. That's essentially what BASE jumping is all about. BASE jumpers get their thrills by jumping at such relatively low altitudes. Instead of 4000 metres from a plane, some BASErs jump from as low as 150 metres off bridges. The danger is the limited amount of time this affords to correct any errors or malfunctions. The BASE jumpers I know tend to be methodical planners and it is this minimizing of risk and the careful preparations that give them a large part of the BASE buzz – as well as, of course, the actual moment of the jump, which is often carried out illegally and at night!

DON'T TRY THIS AT HOME

The word itself is an acronym and stands for the types of objects that people jump from: B is for Buildings; A is for Antennas (aerial masts); S is for Spans (bridges); and E is for Earth (usually meaning cliffs). BASE jumpers have parachutes attached to their back but they don't have much time to open them. That is why so many BASErs pay the ultimate price.

The skill of BASE jumping is in keeping the body stable from the moment of launch so that the parachute opens cleanly and doesn't get snagged either on the object (building, cliff, antenna, etc.) or around the limbs of the jumper. Body stability is easier to achieve the faster you are going but as it takes up to 12 seconds to reach terminal velocity (around 120mph), this is time most BASE jumpers don't have. Unstable or 'off-heading' launches are all too common and often

It's mad, it's bad, and it's very dangerous. But there are people out there who are willing to risk everything for the biggest thrill of them all.

have fatal consequences with the jumper hitting an outcrop from a cliff, for example.

BASE jumpers are awarded a number when they have successfully jumped from one of each of the four categories of fixed object launch pads. Since the awards of BASE Numbers 1 and 2 to Americans Phil Smith and Phil Mayfield in 1981, there are now around 800 'certified' jumpers around the world. Certified insane, some might say.

Toasting the Queen at our record-breaking, high-altitude dinner party, set at 7,500 metres.

CARL BOENISH – THE ORIGINAL BIRDMAN

Carl 'Ronnie' Boenish was a Norwegian freefall photographer and is known as the 'father of BASE jumping'. A skydiving film-maker, he was the first to apply modern technology in the form of ram air parachutes and freefall tracking techniques to the art of leaping off fixed objects.

In 1978 he filmed four friends jumping from the famous cliff face of El Capitan in Yosemite National Park and later produced some of the most thrilling skydiving films ever made. Carl was a casualty of the sport he invented and in 1984 was killed jumping from Norway's Trollveggen, otherwise known as the Troll Wall. In 1987, in recognition of his achievements, he was awarded the USPA Achievement Award, the skydiving community's highest award.

TO BASE OR NOT TO BASE

While BASE jumping is illegal in many parts of the world, there is an increasing number of year-round sites where jumping is both legal and welcome. These include more than seventy cliffs near Moab in Utah, USA as well as others in Italy, Norway, Sweden and Switzerland.

Even some cities have now started to welcome BASE jumpers, including the Malaysian capital, Kuala Lumpur, where BASE jumping competitions are held from the Petronas Twin Towers (452 metres), and Shanghai, where group jumps have been made from the Jin Mao Tower (427 metres).

KJERAG PLATEAU, LYSEFJORD, NORWAY

Overlooking Lysefjord in western Norway, the Kjerag plateau, a 1000-metre vertical granite cliff, is a BASE jumping Mecca. It is also probably the best place in the world to watch the sport.

The plateau is famous for the 'Kjerag Bolten', a huge chockstone wedged into a crack in the mountain, from which the jumpers launch themselves into the unknown.

PERRINE RIVER BRIDGE, TWIN FALLS, IDAHO, USA

Experienced skydivers flock to the Perrine River Bridge to learn the skills of BASE jumping as it's a legal site and has an excellent landing area. It's also the home of Marta Empinotti, one of the sport's most famous athletes with more than eight hundred jumps to her name.

BRIDGE DAY, FAYETTEVILLE, WEST VIRGINIA, USA

The largest extreme sports event in the world, Bridge Day is held every year on the third Saturday in October when more than 200,000 people converge on the New River Gorge Bridge to watch more than 450 BASE jumpers make the 267-metre plunge into the gorge. BASE jumping from the bridge is allowed during a six-hour window from 9 a.m. to 3 p.m. during this one day of the year. Brilliant!

DEFYING GRAVITY – THE WORLD'S HIGHEST BASE JUMP

In one of the all-time examples of how fear and lack of experience can be overcome to achieve the seemingly impossible, in 2006 Australian Heather Swan broke the BASE jumping world record when she jumped in a wingsuit from Mount Meru in northern India, 6604 metres above sea level. She jumped with her husband, Dr Glenn Singleman, who held the previous world record. Her transformation from a corporate executive with no experience of mountains or skydiving to a world record BASE jumper is described in her book, *Defying Gravity, Defying Fear*.

Base jumping –
one of the most
dangerous (and
scary!) things
it's possible to
experience.

Skiing and Tobogga

Coming Down . . . Fast

Off-piste skiing in deep powder. Just you and the mountain. Heaven!

MOUNTAINS CAN BE hard work to climb up, but they are always fun to come down. I have spent a considerable portion of my life going up and down mountains – and they are both entirely addictive, but in different ways.

Climbing up is like a slow, steady, methodical game of chess on a vast scale, edging your way round crevasses and cornices, often wading through waist-deep powder snow, heart thumping, sweat freezing and legs burning. And in the connection between man and mountain there is a quiet sort of solitude. I love that. Coming down is much more dynamic. It's fast, technical, graceful and intuitive. How can you not fall in love with skiing in deep powder snow in big mountains? It just takes a little practice. I have had the privilege over the years of skiing many exciting routes with people who are

such masters that they make my skiing pale into insignificance. So I have learnt only ever to admit to being an 'average' skier – and this normally covers me. I figure it is better to try to over deliver than to over promise.

But like many great outdoor adventures, skiing is not about how good you are, it is about a shared joy of the outdoors – and the more dynamic this is, the better. I find if I'm skiing what I consider a hard route together with a great skier then I raise my game almost without knowing it. It is as if their skill and ability produces a confidence in me that allows me to ski stronger and more dynamically than I might normally do. It is a wonderful feeling where together we become stronger and better. I love the way that mountains can bring that out in us.

Skiing with Jesse, my eldest son. Got to start somewhere!

I once filmed a programme in Alaska. The show was to open with a big helicopter scene, summer skiing, high on the Alaskan glaciers. From the heli the face looked near vertical, riddled with crevasses and almost entirely sheet ice. I was nervous (and wishing I had been given the chance to have a few days' warm-up beforehand!). But instead, this was going to be a one-taker. To make matters significantly worse, the guide in the chopper who would be on the radio to my earpiece, directing my route, was an ex-US ski champion (I had, you'll be pleased to note, told him my skiing was 'average'!)

The heli dropped me on the summit. I clipped in and set off down the gentle bowl leading away from the peak and towards the face. My breathing was fast and shallow. I was scared and

there were a lot of the camera team's faces pressed against the windows of the two filming helicopters. As I moved, the snow felt sticky and heavy underneath and I struggled even to turn gently in it at about 5 mph. My nerves weren't helping my shaking legs at all, nor was the voice in my ear telling me the sheer face was 300 metres ahead now. I skied on. I had to make this work. The chopper hovered beside me. I soon reached the edge of the face. It was time to ski for my life.

I always remember being told that 'being tentative has no power', meaning that in being over-cautious we lose the strength and spontaneity that confidence affords. It is like rugby tackling: when you hold back, you get injured. I have always felt that skiing is especially like this. When you are nervous you lean back, the ski tips come up, the traction goes and the skis shoot away from you. Lean forward, be aggressive and dynamic in your movement and you take back the control.

It's about controlling your own mountain rather than letting the mountain control you. I told myself that, took a deep breath and threw myself onto the sheer face with all my heart and soul. It was a privilege to ski here and I felt myself come alive. Despite a near miss as I skidded across a narrow crevasse, the rest of the face, including a steep chimney ski, was awesome fun. The footage was cool, I survived and the ex-ski champion told me I had done 'just above average'. That was good enough for me!

I also love to ski more calmly with my family. That wonderful sensation as powder snow lifts

Lean forward, be aggressive and dynamic in your movement and you take back the control.

Snowshoes I made from willow branches and string – how people would have travelled through deep snow before skis.

I had skinned a dead yak, eaten its eyeballs and used the fur to keep me warm at night.

you up and you feel like you are floating, bouncing, committed to the slope and truly free as you carve your way down a vast snowy mountain face. These are life moments to savour. And don't be scared of wiping out. I do it masses, and it is just part of getting good. Just think rag-doll, keep relaxed and don't worry, you'll stop eventually!

I have also ski-toured a good deal with friends in the mountains and that shared sense of space, where you have climbed your way out of the valleys and pause for a moment with a perfect ski descent beneath you, is so rewarding. It is just you and the mountain, and that great stillness you feel before you set off down is priceless.

And then to round it all off there is tobogganing. It is less skilful, but still wild! Skiing down icy Alpine bobsleigh tunnels in the middle of the night was pretty good, but the best was in Siberia in mid-December. I had skinned a dead yak, eaten its eyeballs and used the fur to keep me warm at night. The next day I used the warm fur to make a toboggan, wrapped around branches, tied together with strips of skin and paracord. In a few hours it had then frozen solid. It was just big enough to squeeze my body into, I was 2000 metres up some remote peak, the sun was shining, and I went down this mountain like a human rocket!

But when it came to being time to bail out there was so much G-force I couldn't get myself out of this carcass. I eventually managed to throw myself free, smashed my elbow and back and was bruised for a week. So the lesson is, stay in control, use brakes and do repeated runs safely rather than one insane one. But either way, it's always wicked fun.

A SHORT HISTORY OF FOOT PLANKS

Rock art discovered on the fringes of the Arctic and dating back to the end of the last Ice Age show that Stone Age man used primitive skis as much as 4500 years ago. However, back then the necessities of survival far outweighed the potential fun to be had whizzing down slopes at high speed. The earliest skis were used to hunt and as a means of travel through backcountry that would otherwise have been inaccessible.

Scandinavia in general and Norway in particular are recognized as the birthplace of the ski, and the word itself is thought to be derived from an Old Norse word, *skio*, meaning 'a piece of split wood'. And indeed it was in Norway in the 1870s that skiing as we know it today first took root.

The first glimmer of skiing's potential as a sport had begun a century earlier with the invention of 'stick riding' which involved descending slopes on rigid skis using a stick held out behind like a tiller to brake and control the direction of travel. But it was a far from perfect solution to the problem of moving quickly across snow-covered, mountainous terrain.

They had so much class in those days!

Put that in your pipe and smoke it!

And at that time skis were little more than planks of wood with very little flexibility or manoeuvrability.

Sondre Norheim – remembered today as the father of modern skiing – came from a tiny farm in the remote valley of Mordegal in the county of Telemark in southern Norway. Sondre revolutionized ski equipment and techniques so that the foot, in combination with the skis themselves, could be used to both turn and brake. The skis he designed were much shorter than traditional skis, more flexible and narrower in the centre making it easier to both turn and move downhill in a controlled fashion.

The bindings he invented were made from the young tendrils of birch trees twisted into strong cord and the invention of Telemark skiing, the ancestor of almost all modern ski sports, meant that the skier could now control the speed and direction of travel by adjusting bodyweight and the angle of the ski itself on the surface of the snow.

ALPINE SKIING

Alpine skiing is the name given to the downhill variety of recreational skiing enjoyed at winter resorts in mountainous regions all over the world. Fun, fast and furious, this heady cocktail of mountain peaks, snow and gluwein has become a regular winter pick-me-up for literally millions of people.

Alpine skiing grew out of the techniques of Telemark skiing. It was pioneered by British skiers who had learnt to ski cross-country in Norway but had become more interested in the adrenalin-fuelled potential of skiing downhill at speed. It was they who started the first downhill race courses in the Alps, including the very first – the Roberts of Kandahar Challenge Cup – which began in 1911 and is still held annually at Mürren in Switzerland.

These races caught the imagination of a new breed of well-off tourists who had started to visit the Alps during the winter months. New techniques like the 'stem christie' turn had also been developed which gave the skier more control at higher speeds and could be learnt in a relatively short period of time. Perfect for visitors from cities across Europe who only had a few weeks to spare.

After the First World War ski schools sprang up all over the Alps teaching the Arlberg System devised by Austria's national ski champion, Johann Schneider. This taught the newly devised snowplough, the stem turn, and the stem christie in a logical progression and still forms the basis of ski instruction to this day. By the 1930s when the first ski lifts were built, Alpine skiing had become popular all over Europe. The years following the end of the Second World War saw the building of the first purpose-built ski resorts in Austria and Switzerland, which laid the foundations of the worldwide industry we enjoy today.

SKI TOURING

Unlike Alpine skiing, ski touring is the modern version of the traditional form of skiing in use since prehistoric times. Known by various names – backcountry skiing in the US and cross-country in Europe – ski touring is the horizontal version of Alpine skiing.

Crevasse crossing on Everest. Crevasses are one of mountains' biggest hazards.

Ski touring is rapidly gaining in popularity as more and more people look for the true winter wilderness experience away from the busy pistes of the top resorts. Ski tourers are able to enjoy untouched areas of wilderness along with all the hazards of avalanche and difficult terrain that go with it. This is a world where conveniences like ski lifts are left far behind and where human power, as in days gone by, is the sole form of locomotion.

The skis used for wilderness ski touring are usually longer and narrower and made of lighter materials than downhill skis, while the design of the bindings vary considerably depending on the type of terrain to be covered.

TELEMARK

Named after the region of Norway where it was first invented, Telemark skiing is the most traditional form of ski touring and is currently enjoying a renaissance. Telemark bindings allow the heel to remain free so turns on downhill sections – where the inside ski trails behind the outer ski while the heel is kept raised – can be difficult to master for those more used to Alpine techniques. Telemark is particularly effective in steep terrain with synthetic fur known as 'skins' used on the bottom of the skis to aid traction in steep uphill sections.

CROSS-COUNTRY

As in Telemark skiing, cross-country bindings attach the toe to the ski and not the heel. The equipment is generally lighter and less robust than Telemark, but requires less energy and strength to master. Cross-country skis are best suited to first-time ski tourers over flat or rolling terrain. They do not have metal edges – unlike Telemark and Randonnée skis – and so are harder to dig in and can be less stable on steep sections.

The ultimate workout – and a beautiful way to move through the mountains.

RANDONNÉE

Also known as Alpine touring, Randonnée opens up the backwoods and mountain wildernesses to Alpine skiers. There are a number of different ski types and bindings available which allow a combination of Alpine and cross-country techniques to be used. Randonnée bindings can be adapted in situ so that the heel can be kept fixed in place during downhill sections allowing the use of Alpine techniques – including the parallel turn – so familiar to recreational skiers.

Fast . . . and feels even faster when you're that close to the ground.

TOBOGGANING

Toboggans are the ultimate form of mobile fun. And the reason for this is their ultimate simplicity. Just like the toboggan I fashioned out of yak hide on my Siberian adventure, anything that will hold a passenger and has a smooth bottom will do. All that is required then is a liberal quantity of compact snow, and gravity will do the rest.

In Scandinavia toboggans are made of wood, traditionally with a curved front end. Dragged by reindeer or husky dogs, they have been used for centuries and became as much a part of the Victorian Christmas in the UK as mince pies and Father Christmas himself. Nowadays, come a fall of snow, everything from tea trays to bin-liners can be seen hurtling down the nearest snow-covered hills as the squeals of delight of their young and not-so-young passengers pierce the crisp air.

Alpine touring in spectacular mountains is hard to beat.

All that is required then is a liberal quantity of compact snow, and gravity will do the rest.

People will go to ridiculous lengths to impress the ladies.

ST MORITZ TOBOGGANING CLUB AND THE CRESTA RUN

Bobsleighs and sleds are an adaptation of toboggans which increase speed exponentially through the addition of a pair of narrow runners on the bottom surface. This reduces the contact area with the snow and the friction that slows it down.

By the middle of the nineteenth century the resort town of St Moritz in Switzerland had become a popular resort for Europe's aristocracy to spend the summer, but the season was soon to be extended when an enterprising hotel owner called Caspar Badrutt persuaded his guests to stay during the winter months as well.

To keep themselves amused, some of his guests began racing up and down the narrow streets on the sleds used by the boys delivering goods to the hotel. This prompted Badrutt to create a track where they could indulge their passion for the craze without risk to life and limb. The track he created, a U-shaped half tube of ice, was in effect the first purpose-built half-pipe and is still in use today.

A few years later, visiting British army officers built a custom-made sled course between the nearby hamlet of Cresta and St Moritz and started the St Moritz Tobogganing Club. The course was more than a kilometre long with a drop of more than 150 metres and renowned for its lethal bends, including the notorious 'Shuttlecock'. The course was subsequently used in two Winter Olympics and is still known the world over as the famous Cresta Run.

I have run the course several times and it is a blast! On one memorable run down the Shuttlecock Corner I flew out having hit the bend at the wrong angle. In mid-air I heard the commentator shout, 'He's out!', but I held on, the toboggan curled back in and I clung to the rails as it creamed back into the inside wall, giving me a good dose of strained muscles and tendons, before screaming off back down the tunnel. I then heard the commentator announce, 'Sorry, correction, he's back in!' Great fun!

SKELETON

Skeleton racing is the original form of competitive sled racing invented by Badrutt's first winter guests. They came up with a 'skeleton' version of the original delivery boy sled design stripped down to its most basic shape – hence its name – and made of metal. In today's modern version, competitors ride head first with their heads only an inch above the surface of the ice and snow at speeds approaching 80mph. Competitors get the sled moving with the initial 'push' wearing sprinting shoes with spikes and jumping on stomach-down at the 50-metre mark with their hands straight down by their side and their toes pointed.

LUGE

One of the first adaptations of the original bobsleigh was the *luge*, the French word for sled. The 'slider', as the luge's passenger is known, rides flat and feet-first. Steering is controlled by small and precise movements of the shoulders and legs and there are no brakes. Protective clothing is also kept to a minimum to achieve maximum aerodynamics, so crashes can easily be fatal. Top luge riders experience G-forces equivalent to jet fighter pilots and on artificial tracks have reached speeds of more than 85mph. The luge was made an Olympic sport in 1964.

Skeleton racing requires nerves of steel, thighs like mountains and very fast reactions.

The Yukon Quest race is held every February. It takes between 11 and 14 days, with the dogs and the mushers eating and sleeping in temperatures as low as minus 50 degrees.

DOG SLED RACING

Sleds pulled by huskies were used extensively in the American North West by the first pioneers, gold prospectors, traders and mailmen. But by the late twentieth century, mechanization had meant that the traditional sled culture of mountain communities like Canada's Yukon and Alaska in the USA was fast dying out. Happily, in recent decades, sled dog racing – or 'mushing' as it is more popularly known – in races like the Iditarod and the Yukon Quest have gone a long way to reviving this dying art.

IDITAROD

The world's most famous sled dog race – sometimes called the 'Last Great Race on Earth' – the Iditarod was first run in 1973 in an attempt to keep alive the traditions of the Iditarod Trail used by the first pioneers. The 1868-kilometre course – between Anchorage, the Alaskan capital, and Nome, on the western Bering Sea coast – takes between 10 and 17 days to complete and crosses mountain ranges, frozen rivers, dense forest, desolate tundra and huge swathes of windswept coastline.

YUKON QUEST

Dog sleds in Canada's Yukon province were made famous in Jack London's epic survival novel *The Call of the Wild*. The Yukon Quest race, which covers the 1600 kilometres of wilderness terrain between Whitehorse, Yukon and Fairbanks in Alaska, was first run in 1984. Held every February, it takes between 11 and 14 days to complete, with the dogs and the mushers eating and sleeping in the wilderness in temperatures that have sometimes reached as low as minus 50 degrees.

Recently, I was out in Whitehorse, Yukon during the other epic race they have out there – the Yukon river race – and it is wild! I rode the rapids further north in an open canoe and got thrown out in a big Grade 4 rapid. I smashed both my knees and almost came a cropper, but then the Yukon is never meant to be easy!

Kite Making and Kite Flying

Harnessing the Wind

3

Kite surfing – a sport I absolutely love!

KIDS ALWAYS SEEM to have the most fun. But there is no rulebook that says the fun has to stop when you grow over four feet tall. I have inherited from my late father a pretty fierce determination not to grow up where growing up is not needed. And making and flying kites is most definitely one of those areas.

When the wind is mild and steady it is great to take to the skies under a paraglider or parachute. Indeed I have spent many hours of my life waiting and hoping for gentle winds so that I could fly off a mountainside. But when it's too windy to paraglide, it is perfect for kite flying. Where paragliding requires gentle winds to be fun, kite flying requires strong winds. Hence it's impossible to be bored with nature. In fact, my mum always used to say that only boring people got bored!

I was with my best buddy recently, and after lunch we went out to the hay barn, climbing up and over the bales. As it was quite windy one of us had the idea to get the kite out, so we scurried inside to grab some boots and the kite.

Out in the field the wind was stronger than we had thought, but by that stage we were already busily rolling the kite out (and over-excited!). The kite was a massive old two-man buggy kite, which generally doubled pretty well as an improvised normal kite, as long as the wind wasn't too strong.

My friend unfurled it, Jesse, my five-year-old, was clinging onto my leg and I was braced ready for the wind to catch it. And catch it, it did! A particularly powerful gust ripped the kite out of my friend's hands, and I just took off, my wellington boots and me skidding across the wet, muddy field, fighting to keep the kite stable above my head with Jesse still clinging onto my leg for dear life. I then skidded down a ditch, dropped to one knee and inadvertently dived the kite a few degrees. That was all the impetus it required to unleash some serious kite-power. The kite tore free from my hands as it catapulted into the air and within seconds it was snared 20 metres up a giant oak tree, billowing like a castle flag. Jesse and I were caked in mud and everyone was doubled over laughing. As far as Jesse was concerned, it was an all-round great adventure!

Harnessing the power of the wind and driving a power kite through the sky while being safely on the ground is a magical sensation. I love that feeling of channelling nature, and rarely is nature so raw as with the power of the wind.

Kite flying goes back thousands of years. It has been the sport of kings and kids alike. At one extreme fighting kites are still flown competitively with wire lines, while at the other kites provide simple pleasure for countless fathers and sons. When we are on our island home in Wales we fly kites almost every day, as in true Welsh fashion it is invariably windy. One of my favourite photos is of my youngest son, Marmaduke, aged one, staggering along like a drunkard, pulling a kite string through a field, not even looking at it as the kite swirled behind him.

Of course, flying a big kite around is a serious workout, because once filled with moving air being driven across the sky, kites develop a life force of their own. The smallest twitch in the fingers can create massive energy and force. If you don't believe me, try kitesurfing (see below), it's a great sport and something that anyone who enjoys kites should look into.

Making a simple kite yourself needn't take ages, and is really fun to do. A basic kite made out of string, some thin branches, some cloth or an old plastic bag will fly. The key is tying the line at the correct point in what is known as a 'bridle' so it

Jesse, my eldest son, flying his favourite kite.

won't just loop the loop into the ground. Keep testing and adjusting a few centimetres at a time until it is stable, then reel it out. It might be less professional than a power kite and it might not drag you out of the water on a board, but it will make you smile big time, as your creation takes to the sky.

> **Flying a big kite around is a serious workout, because once filled with moving air being driven across the sky, kites develop a life force of their own.**

KITES IN HISTORY

Kites have been around for quite a while, probably more than three thousand years. Although everyone agrees the first kites came from the Far East, exactly where and when they were first flown is lost in the mists of time. One problem for historians is that the earliest examples were made from light, perishable, natural materials – bamboo, wood and silk – and so nothing of them has survived.

One theory is that the earliest kites were made of palm leaves, long before the invention of paper, and used by islanders in the South Pacific for sea fishing. But a popular tradition handed down through oral history is that the first kite-maker, Lu Ban, lived in China in the fourth or fifth century BC. He is said to have made kites in the shape of huge birds that were capable of flying for days at a time.

The first written mention of kite flying dates back to the Han Dynasty (206 BC– AD 220). A Chinese general is said to have used the length of a kite's towline to estimate how far his men would have to dig to tunnel under the walls of a palace his army was besieging. In later centuries, kite flying spread along trade routes throughout Asia to Malaysia, Indonesia, Thailand, Korea and India as well as to the Maoris in what later became New Zealand.

As its popularity grew, each culture developed its own unique styles and rituals of kite making and kite flying. The first kites reached Japan with

Buddhist monks who flew them to ward off evil spirits and ensure a good harvest. Over the centuries kites have been used for a wide range of other purposes including religious ceremonies, military reconnaissance, building construction and scientific research.

The first kites to reach Europe were brought back at the end of the thirteenth century by the explorer Marco Polo, and for many years were used primarily for scientific and military purposes. It was only in France in the early 1700s that they first became popular for recreational flying.

Innovations in kite design followed, most notably the invention in 1893 of the box kite by Lawrence Hargrave, an Englishman who emigrated to Australia, and a man-lifting cell kite designed by Alexander Graham Bell, inventor of the telephone. The Wright brothers used observations of the aerodynamic characteristics of kites and Hargrave's box kite designs to develop plans for their first aeroplanes.

But it was in the late twentieth century that new materials like ripstop nylon, fibreglass and Kevlar were incorporated into revolutionary new designs and paved the way to the modern explosion in the popularity of kite flying. The launch of the Peter Powell stunt kite in 1972, a highly manoeuvrable kite controlled by as many as four towlines instead of the traditional single line, made acrobatic kite flying possible for millions.

KITE TYPES

There are literally thousands of kite designs. At one end of the scale are the popular diamond kites, with tails like a schoolgirl's pigtail, which can be seen dipping and weaving across the sky on any breezy weekend around our coasts. At the opposite end of the scale are the Chinese super-giants in the shape of dragons, serpents and jellyfish flown by teams of grown men barely able to anchor them to the ground.

But however colourful or elaborate they may be, most kites fall into one or other of the following categories:

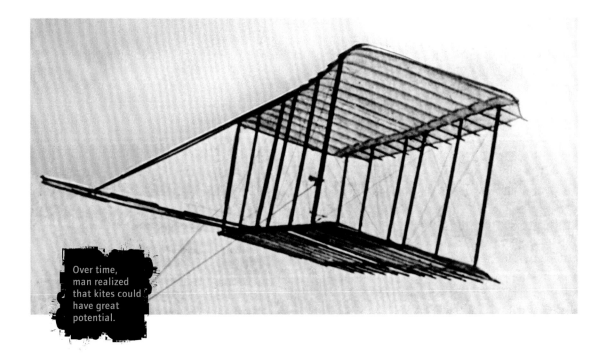

Over time, man realized that kites could have great potential.

BOX OR CELLULAR

Made of box shapes or tetrahedron cells, these three-dimensional kites can be extremely elaborate and eye-catching. They also generate powerful lift and were used by the first aviators. They are best flown in stronger winds but tend to fly at a lower angle than other kites.

DELTA

Triangular in shape with a V-shaped leading edge and a keel for stability, Delta kites are based on the wings invented by the American designer Francis Rogallo. It was his designs that inspired the invention of the hang glider which also have a Delta-type design. Delta kites are extremely flexible as the rods are not joined, allowing the kite to be moulded by the wind, an integral part of its design. They are often constructed in a bird shape and are excellent for flying on low wind days.

SLED

The ultimate foldaway pocket kites, sled kites are designed to flex in the middle with only basic stiffeners running along the length of the kite. Wings on the side provide stability and inflatable cells are sometimes built into the design to prevent wobble. They are best flown in light, steady winds.

PARAFOIL

These kites have no frame but are inflated by the wind, which fills cells stitched into an envelope of fabric like a rectangular windsock. Once inflated, the kite flies in much the same way as the wing of a bird or a plane, generating much more lift than other kite designs. Parafoils are often huge and designed in the shape of animals. Beware the power. I have often been dragged around and dumped in a bush, or worse, by a parafoil kite!

Sports associated with kiting have gone through the roof.

FLAT

The simplest form of kite constructed from a frame with cross spars to hold the structure completely flat and rigid. Shapes vary from the popular diamond, to stars, hexagons or serpents. Flat kites tend to be less stable in flight than other designs and are best flown in medium winds.

BOWED

This design innovation was first introduced in the Eddy kite (see below) and dramatically improves the stability of flat kites by bending the cross spar of the surface that faces the wind into a convex bow. This improves the aerodynamics by keeping the airflow over the front of the kite more steady and giving the kite more lift. Flies well in a wide range of wind speeds.

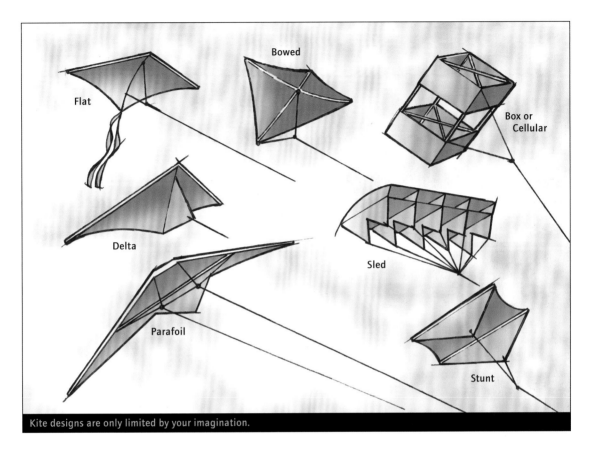

Flat

Bowed

Box or
Cellular

Delta

Sled

Parafoil

Stunt

Kite designs are only limited by your imagination.

STUNT KITES

In 1975, Englishman Peter Powell revolutionized the sport of kite flying when he launched the first stunt kites. These highly manoeuvrable kites with long, inflatable tails are capable of acrobatic displays made possible by additional towlines, which vary the air pressure over the surface of the kite. Complex acrobatic displays at high speeds are now relatively easy to perform.

MAKING A KITE

This Eddy kite is a variation on the standard diamond or lozenge kite designs that have been popular in Europe for centuries. It is a 'bowed' kite with a convex curve on the cross spar which makes it much more stable in the air than the standard flat design. The original design was patented in 1900 by William Eddy, an American accountant and journalist, who wanted to build a kite that could lift meteorological and photographic equipment into the air.

The aerodynamic qualities of the design were such a success that multiple combinations or 'trains' of Eddy kites were later used to lift weather instruments to heights of more than 7000 metres, an altitude record that stood for many years.

The secret of making a successful Eddy kite is to make sure the measurements are exact and the result symmetrical. The first task is to construct the frame. At this stage you will need to decide the size of the kite you want to make. This will depend largely on the materials you have available,

the space you have to store it, and whether it can be easily carried to your chosen flying site. Remember, the bigger it is the higher it may go, but the less manoeuvrable it will be in flight.

MATERIALS

The main ingredients needed to build a successful kite are patience, space, and the right equipment and materials. The contents of a standard toolbox will usually supply the most important items: a pencil, ruler, scissors, a sharp knife, set square and a hacksaw.

The simplest kites can be made out of lightweight paper, bin liners or ripstop nylon for the sail with the frame made of bamboo, wooden or fibreglass rods. Glue, adhesive tape and nylon fishing line are all that are needed to hold the basic structure together, but kite shops stock all sorts of useful connections and fastenings like plastic rings, joints and tubing which all make construction easier, lighter and stronger. Towlines need to be strong enough not to snap under tension, but light enough to allow the structure to fly.

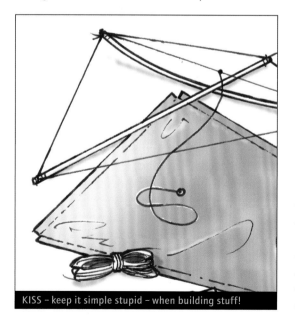

KISS – keep it simple stupid – when building stuff!

The simplest kites can be made out of lightweight paper, bin liners or ripstop nylon for the sail.

CONSTRUCTION

The two rods of the cross-shaped central frame should be exactly the same length. I would suggest using rods one metre long and about half a centimetre thick, depending on the strength and flexibility of your materials. Use a sharp knife to cut a small circular notch around both ends of each rod where the nylon cord can be tied with a round turn and two half hitches (see p. 250).

Tie a piece of nylon cord to one end of one rod and pull it taut around the other end so that the rod bends into a bow shape. Tie it off leaving a gap of about 10cm – about a tenth of the height of the kite – between the cord and the bow of the rod at its widest point.

Next, lash the bowed rod and the straight rod together in a cross-shape so that they join halfway across the horizontal bowed rod and 20cm from the top of the vertical rod (i.e. around a fifth of the way down from the top). Make sure they are exactly at right angles. (Use a stopping knot for this. Twice around the sticks, tie an overhand knot in the loose end and then tie that whole loose end in another overhand knot around the main length of rope. This will tighten itself and not slide through.)

Then tie another piece of cord (in a round turn and two half hitches) to the top end of the vertical rod and, keeping it as taut as possible, tie it to each rod end in turn making the outline of a diamond. Now lay the diamond shape on the material you are using for the sail and mark out the outline of the frame leaving a margin of about a centimetre all the way round. Cut it to shape and fold it around the frame, gluing, or preferably stitching it, firmly in place while keeping the materials as taut as possible.

The cord that makes the 'bridle' – which attaches the kite to the towline – should be about 1.5 metres in length (i.e. one-and-a-half times the height of the kite). Attach one end of the bridle cord to the front of the kite. Then tie a plastic ring (about half a centimetre in diameter) about half a metre along the bridle cord and the other end to the bottom of the kite. The towline can then be attached to the plastic ring and your Eddy kite will be ready to fly.

To make the kite more stable and dramatic in flight, a tail made of connecting rings or strips of material can be attached to the bottom of the kite.

POWER KITES

Many modern kite designs are so efficient that they can generate enough power to pull a grown man off his feet and into the air. And not surprisingly, inventors have long wanted to harness the power of kites to pull vehicles across the land and surfboards across the sea. These are known as power or traction kites and include everything from kite buggies to windsurfers, kite skateboards and snowkites.

Many modern kite designs are so efficient that they can generate enough power to pull a grown man off his feet and into the air.

Be careful, there is huge power in kites.

GEORGE POCOCK AND THE CHARVOLANT

Today when you see a kite buggy being pulled along a beach or a kitesurfer skipping over the waves, it's easy to forget that the inspiration behind these amazing inventions was a nineteenth-century schoolteacher and inventor from Bristol called George Pocock, who invented a kite-drawn carriage called a 'charvolant' or 'flying carriage'.

After experimenting with large boards and planks (and then on his children with chair-lifting kites), in 1826 he patented the design for a kite-drawn carriage. The kite was controlled by a driver paying out four lines from spools mounted on the front of the carriage and could reach speeds of 20mph both down- and upwind.

He wrote in rapturous tones in 1827, 'Harnessing the invincible winds, our celestial tandem playfully transpierces the clouds, and our mystic moving car swiftly glides along the surface of the scarcely indented earth'. Elsewhere, he also records that one of his charvolants beat a horse-drawn mail coach from Bristol to Marlborough in a race while on another occasion he incurred the wrath of the Duke of Gloucester when his charvolant overtook the Duke's carriage.

KITESURFING

Few adventure sports come near to the thrill of kitesurfing. A hybrid combination of many other sports including surfing, wakeboarding, paragliding and kite flying, kitesurfers use the power of the wind to propel themselves over the surface of the water.

As with all kite sports, a good level of proficiency is needed to judge the power of the wind and keep both the kite above you and the board attached to your feet under control. (I am a self-confessed addict of this sport!) Due to their

I told you, it's hard not to smile!

er Lynn with one of his fun designs – what a cool job!

aerodynamic properties, kitesurfers can be flown in winds of less than ten knots and generate great power, something which novices ignore at their peril.

Kitesurfing took off internationally in the 1990s following the launch of a Leading Edge Inflatable (LEI) kite called the Wikipa kite designed in France by the Legaignoux brothers. This innovative design – with an inflatable leading edge – meant that for the first time, the kite element could be easily relaunched after dropping in the water, a problem that is almost inevitable even for the most experienced kitesurfers.

PETER LYNN

One of the most charismatic figures in modern kite design is the New Zealander Peter Lynn. As well as designing and building some of the largest display kites in the world for international festivals, including the famous spar-less kites based on marine creatures including the Stingray and Octopus kites, he also invented the first kite buggies and effectively kick-started the modern craze for kite-powered craft on land, sea and ice. Many of Lynn's designs have been used for polar crossings and one of his most recent inventions, the KiteSled, was used to make a 700-kilometre crossing of the Greenland icecap.

He also invented the first kite buggies and effectively kick-started the modern craze for kite-powered craft on land, sea and ice.

. . . and they come in massive sizes like this!

Free power, the best sort.

KITE RECORDS

LARGEST
As well as pioneering power kiting, Peter Lynn also designed the largest kite ever flown. The MegaFlag is 40 metres wide and 24.5 metres deep, and when fully inflated fills an area of more than 930 square metres.

FASTEST
The fastest recorded kite speed is more than 120mph.

HIGHEST
The record for the highest single kite flown is 3801 metres, and for a train of kites 9739 metres. That's over 900 metres higher than the summit of Mount Everest.

HEAVIEST
Some Japanese kites weigh in at more than 2 tonnes.

LONGEST
The longest single kite flight was recorded at 180 hours.

Tree Clim and Tr Houses

Hanging Out in the Trees

The more I experience animals and nature, the more amazed I am.

THE MORE I learn about trees, the more I am in awe of them. Did you know that the main life in a tree is in the outer inch of its bark, and the rest of it is really just its history? That's why trees can be hollow but still vibrant. Did you know that some trees react to what is happening to them? For example, the mopane tree in Africa will only allow elephants to graze from its leaves for about 15 minutes at a time before it secretes tannin into the leaves to deter them from stripping it bare. Now, I'm not the tree-hugger type, but for me trees really do rock, and people who diss trees obviously need to mess around in them more often!

By the way, talking of messing around, I know of a poison apple tree in the jungles of Panama, which if you so much as sleep near it, will cover you in an agonizing rash, and if you eat from it you will die. So, my advice is never underestimate a tree!

Which brings me on to how cool trees are to hang out in or build a house in, and I have had the good fortune to do both of those things on a regular basis.

When I was a kid trees were my escape, and I have been climbing them as far back as I can remember. At the end of our garden we had one particularly good maple tree that over time I became pretty darn good at swinging through and diving around. I could climb 20 metres up it in a matter of seconds, and my route down was even faster. To me, my time in that tree was heaven. I had peace and quiet, I could watch everything going on around our small village ...

People who diss trees need to mess around in them more often!

and I could escape the chores! That tree was also where I used to go to open the letters containing my exam results. And trust me, those moments required plenty of calm!

At school I was also surrounded by some serious monster trees. One of the big branches of a particular tree was so long and bendy that I could crawl along it and it would arch downwards and drop me onto another branch that would swing me across to another tree. I loved the feeling of knowing that I could move fast and safely through the branches up above the world, hidden by leaves from below. I felt invisible and in control.

One of the great pleasures of those big school trees was showing my friends around my territory in the sky and messing about together high up in the branches . . . The other great pleasure was getting my first kiss in one! And I have loved trees ever since.

As I write I can look out of my window and see a half-built tree house that we are making for my two boys and me. Well, if something is fun, why give it up?! In my view not nearly enough adults either climb trees or build tree houses – and boy are they missing out.

> These days, particularly in the US, **TREE CLIMBING** is becoming a popular sport offered by commercial companies. Some people are also pushing the envelope. There is one particular branch of the sport that is not for the faint-hearted. Some particularly adventurous and skilled tree climbers get their kicks from limb surfing, walking to the end of a high branch and letting the wind bounce them around. All while roped in, of course.
>
> You see . . . trees really do rock.

My two sons in our tree house – and I think they like it.

The higher you get, the more fun it becomes.

ADVENTURES IN TREE WORLD

Kids love trees. Climbing them, playing in them, even building houses in them appeals to their natural sense of adventure. It takes them into a parallel universe and is often their first experience of looking down on the world from above. This, no doubt, explains why so many children's adventure books, from *Jack & the Beanstalk* to Enid Blyton's *Magic Faraway Tree* and JRR Tolkien's *Lord of the Rings*, involve such memorable trees.

Trees are like people. They have different personalities and different shapes. Some are tall and straight like pines, while others, like oaks and elms, can be gnarled and sinuous with branches that zigzag towards the heavens. Things look different from up a tree. Up close and personal, in among their branches and leaves, you can find a whole new world of sight, sound, smell and touch. And time passes differently up there in the sky. With a panoramic view of the world, you can see without being seen – another big attraction for an adventurous kid.

TO CLIMB OR NOT TO CLIMB

Choosing the right tree to climb is as much of an art as a science. Some trees just scream out to be climbed, while others have more subtle qualities that might not be so obvious at first. Often your chosen tree will be one you are familiar with. And if it's in your own garden so much the better because you won't need to ask permission to climb it. If on the other hand you choose to climb a tree in the middle of a forest, the experience will be very different.

When making your choice it's important to remember that height isn't everything. Trees come in all shapes and sizes. Those with branches that are thick and wide and spread generously but are evenly spaced will often be better than ones that are tall with branches that are far apart. The dense foliage of an evergreen will also feel very different from a deciduous tree and won't have such good views.

Have a long look at any tree you are thinking of climbing and beware of rushing in before you've sized things up. Examine it carefully both from a distance, where you will get a wide-angle view, and then close-up. Walk around it for a full 360-degree view and note how the branches are spaced out on the trunk. Divide it up into three zones: the roots and the base of the tree; the trunk in the main central section; and finally the crown at the top.

The first thing to ask yourself is whether the tree is leaning. If it is, you may get a very special view at the top, but it could also come crashing down with you in it. The roots and the ground around the tree will soon tell you whether or not it is dangerous. Clear away any leaves or debris to check that the surrounding ground is not cracked. Then make sure there is no daylight between the roots and the earth and that there is no rot caused by fungus, all of which could mean the tree is in danger of being uprooted. Dead branches on the ground are also a bad sign.

Further up, look for cavities or a split in the trunk, which may mean it has been struck by lightning. In the top half of the tree, be particularly cautious of dead limbs, which often mean the tree is dying, whereas dead branches further down can just be caused by lack of light. And remember – never climb dead trees.

Kids love trees. Climbing them, playing in them, even building houses in them appeals to their natural sense of adventure.

Using three roots of a giant tree to get down into a volcanic lava tube.

It's not just Tarzan who can enjoy swinging around in trees.

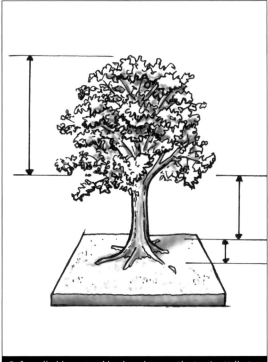

Before climbing, stand back and assess the tree's attributes.

The double rope technique for tree climbing.

TREE CLIMBING TECHNIQUES

Free climbing – without the aid of ropes or harnesses – is often the most fun way of climbing a tree. But you need to be sure its branches are thick and strong with lots of clefts and natural platforms for your hands and feet because the higher you get, the higher the penalty for falling becomes. Which is where roped climbing, using techniques borrowed from rock climbers and potholers, really comes into its own.

DOUBLE ROPE TECHNIQUE

This is the most widely used roped tree-climbing method. One end of a rope is attached to a climber's harness while the other end is thrown over a branch (or even fired with a crossbow if the climb is really high), with a weighted pouch called a throw bag and a throw line (a thinner rope which makes it easier to pull the climbing rope down into position) attached to the end.

Then a first klemheist knot (see p. 250), a type of friction knot, is tied from your harness onto the rope that has been thrown over the branch. This tightens when the climber puts his weight onto it but can slide up the rope when the weight is taken off. Then a second, longer klemheist is tied below the first knot, and this acts as a foot loop that again can slide up but not down. Stand on the foot loop and then slide the top klemheist up as high as it will go. Then rest your weight in the harness and reach down and slide the bottom klemheist up, stand in it and repeat the process.

It takes some practice to find the rhythm but the key is taking your time, conserving energy and letting the knots take the strain, not your muscles.

SINGLE ROPE TECHNIQUE

This technique involves the climber ascending a single piece of rope attached to a high branch. To attach the rope to the branch, first make a small loop in one end tied off with a bowline before throwing the other end over the branch with a throw bag. After removing the throw bag, push the free end through the loop and pull tight around the branch like a hangman's noose.

Using a mechanical ascender – two one-way metal handles that can be pushed up the rope when no weight is applied but which lock shut when the climber's weight is pulling down – the climber now moves steadily up using a 'push me, pull you' motion. This involves pulling with the arms and pushing with the legs so that the climber is alternately standing and then sitting.

This method can be easier for beginners as it makes more use of the legs and is less exhausting. The drawback, however, is that a different set-up needs to be in place for the descent. This is quite complicated to do and can therefore be risky for a novice.

The single rope technique makes good use of the climber's legs.

TREE CLIMBING

It's very important to make sure that both you, and the tree, remain safe and unharmed while climbing. Always use the type of specialist arborist rope used by tree surgeons and not a rock climbing rope. The latter is a 'static' rope and will not produce the friction required by the double rope technique.

As well as a helmet, rope and harness, a cambium saver should also be used. This consists of two steel rings fixed to each end of a flat

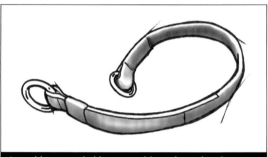

A cambium saver holds a rope without damaging the tree.

webbed strap. This is attached to the rope at the point where it wraps around the tree. It provides static and stops the bark being damaged.

HAMMOCKS AND TENTS

Once they've discovered the joys of clambering around in trees, kids often find that they are better at climbing trees than their parents. This is a great confidence builder in itself. And once a particular tree has become a familiar friend, it becomes a great place to relax, make a den and get away from it all. That's when spending a night up there under a full moon with the sounds of night creatures and the hooting of owls becomes hard to resist.

It's hard to beat this as a place to spend the night.

These days there are all sorts of tree hammocks and tents you can buy. Tree boats are four-cornered hammocks that can be suspended from the branches. They are specially designed for use in trees and so are perfectly safe and very comfortable as long as the occupant remains firmly attached to the tree by a rope and harness. Tree tents are much the same but have a canvas roof to keep you dry when it rains.

But (and so much better) with a little bit of effort and imagination you can build yourself a tree house.

Tree boats are hammocks suspended from branches.

TREE HOUSES

There are an infinite variety of structures you can build in a tree and no two are ever the same, which is a special part of their appeal. A lot will depend on the size and shape of the tree (or trees) that you decide to build in, but remember, the standard square construction is not the only possibility.

DESIGN

Tree houses with an adventurous theme are always popular with kids and there are many possibilities: from pirate ship houses complete with mast and rigging to forts, crow's nest-type constructions with a one-man look-out platform high up and houses with platforms on different levels. A tree house can also be built across one, two or even three trees as long as they are close enough together. The design and look of a tree house will very much depend on the tree in which it is being built. Using the shape of the tree – in particular the branches – as part of the construction is all part of the fun. You're limited only by your imagination.

WHICH TREES MAKE GOOD HOMES?

The most important consideration before you start is to choose a tree that is strong enough to take the weight of the tree house and will not be damaged by having Robin Hood and his band of Merry Men on board. Oaks and beeches are excellent candidates as are ash, cedar and mature fruit trees, but you need to make sure the latter are on a big enough scale. Normally, for any significant structure, this means finding a tree whose trunk is half a metre in diameter with thick, sturdy branches. Also, don't fall into the trap of thinking a tree house in the heavens is the be-all and end-all. A tree house that's close to the ground will actually be a lot easier to build and maintain and will consequently be a lot safer.

Some people always take it too far.

CONSTRUCTION

The most important part of any construction is to put a strong, level platform in place first. This is often easier in trees with a straight trunk where any significant forks are above the level of the platform. This way you can decide on the shape or theme of your tree house without branches getting in the way. The only downside is that the platform will be much harder to support, as it will not be using a fork in the trunk to bear the weight. This can be overcome with careful bracing. While they may be harder to design, the 'perfect' trees for building tree houses are those that have thick branches leaving the trunk at the same level or have a fork in the trunk providing a firm base for a platform.

A platform doesn't need to be square but it does need to be level. A good technique for this is to take a plank between 1½ and 2 metres long and a spirit level up into your chosen tree and mark out where the platform will best sit flat on the branches. You will then need to construct at least three supports that will hold the platform beams firmly in place.

Allowing some flexibility in the joints where the structure is directly connected to the tree is also important as trees flex and bend in high winds, so

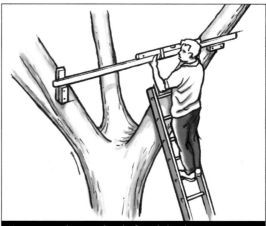

You must make sure the platform is level.

Position the platform carefully and safely.

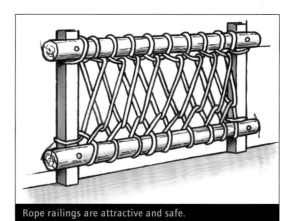

Rope railings are attractive and safe.

the tree house will need to 'give' a little. Diagonal bracing across the bottom of the platform and from the trunk of the tree itself to the edges will also considerably strengthen it. Also remember that if you have a veranda outside the main construction, railings are vital for safety reasons. You can use wood for these but rope railings made properly will be just as safe and look far better.

Once the platform is in place, the shape and design of a tree house and its features from doors and windows to verandas, thatched roofs, secret trap doors, ladders, spiral staircases around the trunk (or in it!), slides, swings, rope bridges, escape hatches and flag poles is up to you to dream up.

CELEBRITY TREES

The infinite variety of trees never ceases to amaze me. Of all living organisms, they are surely the most diverse in the range of shapes and sizes they can eventually grow into. The tallest, like California's giant redwoods, regularly grow to more than 100 metres in height (taller than London's Big Ben), the trunks of baobab trees in Africa and Australia have been known to exceed 150 metres in diameter, while the oldest known living tree ever discovered was a bristlecone pine called Prometheus (see below), estimated to be nearly 5000 years old.

HYPERION

The world's tallest living tree, nicknamed Hyperion, was discovered in 2006 in a remote area of California's Redwood National Park but its exact location has been kept a secret to protect it and others in the near vicinity. It stands 115.5 metres tall.

PROMETHEUS

The oldest known living tree, bristlecone pine Prometheus, grew on Wheeler Peak in what is now Great Basin National Park, Nevada. Crazily, it was chopped down in 1964 to discover its age (around 4900 years old). When this act of scientific vandalism was discovered, it understandably caused outrage. Happily, the exact location of Methuselah, a bristlecone pine growing in California's White Mountains and now the oldest known living tree, at about 4600 years old, is a closely guarded secret.

ANCIENT OAK TREES

Ancient oaks hold a special place in the affections of many people for their majestic presence and the incredible shapes and contortions they develop after many hundreds of years of growth. Among the most famous in the UK are the Major Oak of Sherwood Forest, the Bowthorpe Oak in Lincolnshire, the Majesty in Kent and Old Knobbley in Essex.

The Major Oak is these days a venerable old soldier held up by supports under its huge branches while the Bowthorpe Oak, thought to be over 1000 years old, still stands in a grassy meadow behind a 400-year-old farmhouse. It is rumoured to have once held 39 people at one time. The Majesty in Kent, said to be the most impressive of all British oaks, has a hollow trunk with a circumference of 40 feet. Old Knobbley is the only one of the four that can still be safely climbed.

Oh, and by the way, remember never to ring-bark a tree (which is where you remove a ring of bark from around the trunk). I have watched people do this inadvertently while standing, chatting at the base of a tree. Ring-barking a tree will kill it . . . dead!

Ancient oaks hold a special place in the affections of many people.

Try not being inspired by something this tall . . . or this old (see opposite)!

Playing Games
Letting Off Steam the Natural Way

WHY DO people think that when they grow up they must also stop having fun?! Almost every kid can do a handstand but I can count on about three fingers the number of grown-ups I know who can still do them. Handstands are fun, as are break falls and hanging upside down by your knees (something that I do still almost every day to the dismay of our neighbours). But as a kid I never aspired to being either sensible or smart, and as a grown-up I try my damnedest to be neither.

We all get just one life and there is too much fun to be had in this world messing about with friends in mountains, rivers and lakes to give it

all up on the illusion of having to be 'grown up'. When I reached eighteen I made a firm commitment to myself to keep smiling, laughing, playing and improvising for the rest of my days, and boy am I glad I did.

If you stop using it, you are liable to lose it, and like Peter Pan that sense of wonder and adventure and playfulness is much harder to rekindle once the fire has gone out (though, of course, it's not impossible!). So wherever you are, put your pride to one side, put your ego away, let your hair down and commit to some proper playfulness and games! And if it takes a kid close to you to encourage you to do this, then

all the better. The day you become too proud to learn from children is a seriously bad day!

In this day and age a lot of kids lose their playfulness and imagination too young. Computer games often suck life and imagination dry. They don't require us to improvise. We lose that ability to play with one toy in a thousand different ways. Travelling the world and watching kids in poor, remote villages play is one of life's great lessons. Their toys are never expensive, never plastic and always look such fun. Take wire kite flying in Afghanistan or conkers played with old animal skulls in South America. That's what I call cool!

I have played games in some truly bizarre situations: from I Spy while waiting for a storm to pass stuck in a tent on Everest, to Sardines

Neil and I even played games at 8000 metres on Everest.

while snowed-up in a remote tea-house in the foothills of the Himalayas. I remember being in the middle of Africa with some friends once. We rigged up a slack line slung between army Land Rovers and devised balancing games while waiting to be picked up from a remote airfield.

Jesse joining in one of my outdoor workouts. He's so ridiculous!

I have made improvised swings over jungle rivers that were too wide to cross and played Hide-and-Seek in desert canyons and caves. DIY games are both fun and satisfying. Go and make a football out of cardboard and gaffer tape and see who can bounce it on their feet the most times, or design some makeshift skis to take out into the garden on a frosty morning.

A healthy amount of messing about is even more essential when a lot of your work time is high pressure and intense. We all need to let off

> **A healthy amount of messing about is even more essential when a lot of your work time is high pressure and intense.**

steam and the natural way (i.e. to play) is always the healthiest option. Heart pounding, belly laughing, mind-whirring, it is all good for the soul, so enjoy these ideas for a summer or winter's day wherever you are. And remember, all the great men and women of the world know how to play, from Peter Pan and Robin Hood to Nelson Mandela and Princess Diana. Playfulness enriches life, and after all life is meant to be fun!

ROPE SWINGS

Swings are definitely fun. And anyone who ever jumped out of a plane with a parachute on their back or leapt off a bridge with a bungee cord attached to their legs almost always started their flying days on a swing. Swings are where kids first squeal with delight, their tummies dissolving into a squidgy whirlpool of sensations as they fly towards the sun one moment before being

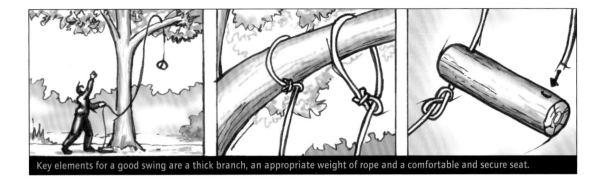

Key elements for a good swing are a thick branch, an appropriate weight of rope and a comfortable and secure seat.

plucked back down to earth by gravity's hairy hand the next.

The best trees for swings are ones that grow on the side of a steep bank with a long, strong branch that stretches out at least three metres above and along the length of the slope. These will give the most intense sensation and thrill of flying through space, but at the same time have the worst penalty if the branch or rope snaps. Make absolutely sure that the tree is healthy and that the branch is strong and thick enough to take repeated strain. Use the type of rope

designed to take heavy weights, like those used by tree surgeons or rock climbers.

If the branch cannot be reached by climbing, attach a weighted 'throw bag' to one end of the rope and throw it over the branch so the two ends of the rope are hanging down beside you. Then tie a bowline in one end and thread the other end through the loop and pull it tight around the branch like a hangman's noose.

At this point, you can decide whether to go for a Tarzan-type swing – it'll be much more comfortable if you wear gloves – or to add a seat

No peeking means no peeking!

Dad, you're so slow!

by tying a second rope a little bit further along the branch and parallel to the first with a branch to sit on tied between them.

You can also just tie the end in a giant ball of granny knots to make it large enough to sit on, or tie the rope around the centre of a hefty metre-long length of wood that will be the seat that goes between your legs. This can be further secured by putting a few nails through the knot and into the piece of wood. (Use a round turn and two half hitches (see p. 251) to attach the knot initially.)

TAG GAMES

Tag, It, and other chase games are among the oldest outdoor games in existence and have been a staple of playgrounds around the world for centuries. The essential format – one player chasing the others until they are tagged or touched and so join the chasing team or are out of the game – has a whole host of different permutations.

Chase games are best played in a reasonably large area with five or more players, hiding places in the form of undergrowth, trees or rocks are an essential ingredient. This means that guile – rather than just the pure speed and agility needed in wide-open spaces – can be brought into play. Tag games are a great way of breaking the ice with a group of children (or adults) who may not know each other well and a perfect way of burning off excess energy!

IT

This is the simplest form of the game. One player is designated 'It' and has to chase the others until he touches another player who then takes over. Variations include having to step on another player's shadow (can cause disputes) or 'Sticky Toffee Pudding' where the player who is 'It' has to chase the others with one hand stuck to the point where he or she was touched by the previous player. As you can imagine, this can have hilarious results.

STUCK IN THE MUD

This is a similar game to Tag except this time when you are caught you have to stand still with your legs apart as if you were 'stuck in the mud'. You can be freed by one of your fellow players crawling through your legs – but they risk getting tagged in the process. This is my personal favourite Tag game! Can the catcher get everyone standing still with their legs apart?!

123 HOME

If the terrain is right (with lots of trees and bushes) this can be one of the most exciting chase games. Nominate a base point (it may be a tree or a rock) and ask for a volunteer to be 'It'. While the latter closes his or her eyes and counts slowly to 100, the others all melt silently into the undergrowth to hide. Those who are hiding then have to creep forward, using all the available cover, then when they think they are close enough to risk a run for home they break cover and sprint back to the base point and touch it shouting '123 Home' when they get there. If, on the other hand, they are spotted before they can make it home, the player who is 'It' has to sprint back to base and touch it shouting '123 X (player's name)' who then takes no further part in the game. Quiet and stealth over speed and timing!

KIM'S GAME

This is a game with a history. It was originally invented by Rudyard Kipling in his novel *Kim*, and later quoted in Robert Baden-Powell's classic book *Scouting for Boys*, published in 1908. Kipling's book is set at the time of British rule in India, where Kim – the orphaned son of a sergeant in an Irish regiment – grows up on the streets and passes for a young Hindu boy who becomes the disciple of a Tibetan lama. But after being arrested by his father's old regiment on suspicion of being a thief and later taken under their wing, he finds himself enlisted into the world of British espionage where he has to play this game to improve his observational skills.

All you need is something flat, like a tray, and a piece of cloth – a T-shirt will do just fine. One of the party should walk around camp picking up let's say twenty small random objects like stones, pen knives, keys, tea bags or items of cutlery. The objects are then placed on the tray and covered by the cloth. When everyone is ready, take away the cloth and count slowly to 60 while everyone studies the objects in front of them. The cover is then put back over the items and everyone tries to remember them. The one who remembers the most wins.

There are a number of variations on the game (ready for when someone seems to be getting too good), which usually generate a bit of extra excitement. In Blind Kim's Game, everyone shuts

Kim's Game: easy to organize, easy to play and great fun!

their eyes – or are blindfolded if they really can't be trusted – and the objects are handed around so the competitors can identify and subsequently try to remember them only by touch and smell. (This game is great for developing our other senses that can come in so handy in the wild.)

ASTRONOMY GAMES

As our ancestors knew only too well, there is no more fertile playground than the sky at night. Using observation games to free the imagination and increase everyone's knowledge of the night sky is a sure-fire hit. These days, when so many kids live in light-polluted cities and their knowledge of the sky at night is often restricted to a dim awareness that there's something called a moon, an encounter with the mysteries of the universe can sometimes be life-changing.

One great way of starting the evening off is to teach everyone the words to Eric Idle's 'Galaxy Song' and get a sing-song going. Google the lyrics – permission to print them was impossible to get!

The song is funny, easy to learn, hilarious to perform, and full of all the most important facts about our solar system and the universe, which are almost impossible to remember without it. And by and large, the information is as accurate as you will need outside a university lecture hall.

When you've sung it a few times, find a clearing with an unobstructed view of the sky, as far as possible from any light sources like torches or the campfire. Then get everyone to lie down in a big circle with their head towards the centre and their feet pointing outwards. (If someone has remembered to build a totem pole earlier in the day in the middle of the circle, then so much the better.)

Now point out the most important celestial objects in the night sky visible to the naked eye. The moon, the planets and easy-to-recognize constellations like the Plough and Orion should come first. You'll be surprised how many people don't understand the difference between a star and a planet. Point out places like Orion's Sword where other whirlpool galaxies like our own can be seen through a telescope.

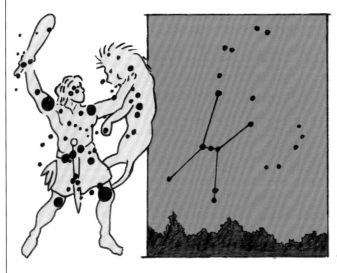
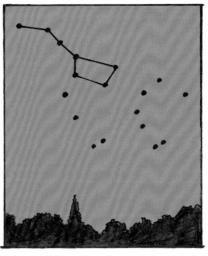

Identifying the constellations in the night sky, like Orion (left) and the Plough (right), makes for a brilliant game.

Now sing that song again . . .

Once you've got everyone looking at the stars with new eyes, have a quiz to see who can spot the most constellations and then get everyone to find the North Star.

FINDING NORTH

First trace the outline of the Plough, then show how the two ends of the 'handle' stars point towards the North Star. Once everyone's located it, find nearby Cassiopeia (it looks like a big W) and show how all the constellations move around the North Star like a giant clock – it's the only star in the night sky that remains in the same place. Then point out Orion: his shoulders, belt and sword are the most prominent features. Show how an imaginary line through his sword and up through the middle of his head also points towards the North Star. You can also explain that this is a good method for finding north in the southern hemisphere when the Plough is no longer in view.

SNOW GAMES

The number of games that can be played in the snow is as limitless as the imagination of those

Games in the snow always end up being funny!

who play them. A whole industry, as we saw in the chapter on skiing and tobogganing, has been built on snow sports with a plethora of new and hybrid sports from snowboarding to snow kiting being invented every year.

But in a situation where there are no skis, no hills, no toboggans and the snowman has already been built, there are still all sorts of options with which to experiment. One of the best is to split into two teams to see who can make the biggest snowball by rolling a small one into a larger one. The trick is to compact the original tiny snowball hard enough to make sure it won't fall apart as it gets bigger. Once a critical mass has been reached, momentum soon takes over and the bigger it gets, the faster it grows.

CONKERS

Like all the best games, the origins of the game of conkers are lost in the mists of time although apparently it used to be played with hazelnuts before horse chestnut trees were brought to Britain. And I am reliably informed that the first record of the game being played in the UK was on the Isle of Wight (where I was brought up) early in Queen Victoria's reign.

Whatever its origins, the game of conkers is now as traditional a part of autumn as strawberries and cream in summer. There is even a World Conker Championship, which is held every year on the second Sunday in October in the village of Ashton, in Northamptonshire in the UK.

The object of the game – as any kid with fire in his belly well knows – is to smash your opponent's conker to smithereens before holding your own up for the same treatment. And this wonderfully British aspect of fair play (combined with some good honest aggression) is what I like about the game so much.

The first, and equally fun, part of the whole process is to find, choose and prepare the perfect fighting conker. It's definitely best to find conkers that have fallen naturally from the tree – unripe ones will still be soft with creamy flecks on the case – and while a really large one may well be a champion in the making, the key thing is to ensure it's fully formed inside and hasn't shrivelled away. The best way to do this is to gather as many as you can and put them in a bucket of water. All the good conkers will sink to the bottom, but those with air spaces will float and should be discarded immediately.

The temptation to artificially harden your conker is hard to resist sometimes, but if you do it's best to come clean and play against opponents who have had a chance to do the same. There are lots of methods – soaking in vinegar, baking in the oven, or covering in nail varnish to name but a few. I used to try the vinegar one at school and the whole sport of conkers was taken very seriously by us eight-year-olds. The prize was chocolate and that was worth fighting for. But if you're thinking long term, leave them in a dark cupboard for a year, as ancient, gnarly ones are always tough to beat. One ex-champion apparently suggests feeding them whole to a pig and then retrieving them suitably hardened when they re-emerge from the other end. Interesting!

However you choose to prepare your conker, it's best to drill a hole in it before you treat it because it's much more likely to splinter after it's been hardened. Drill the hole as near to the centre as you can get and use as sharp a skewer as you can find. Be very careful you don't drill a hole through your hand when the point suddenly emerges from the other side. (Tent pegs can do the job despite being blunt but a small pick on a penknife works best.)

The string should be long enough to wrap around your fingers a few times and hang down between about 20–25 centimetres. Shoelaces are perfect for this as the ends are far easier to push through and knot. Then toss a coin to decide who hits first. Before you strike, wrap the string around your fingers so you have a firm purchase. The holder must then let his conker hang perfectly still at a height to be decided by the hitter, who then has three strikes before the roles are reversed. This continues until one of the conkers is destroyed and the other declared the winner.

There are a number of theories as to whether it's best to hit down on the top of the conker or to swipe it from the side. Arguably the latter makes contact with the softer part of the case, but it's also more difficult to get an accurate hit. Variations include the rule of 'strings' whereby, if the strings get tangled, the first person to shout 'strings' gets an extra shot. An extra shot can also be awarded if the striker manages to hit his opponent's conker so hard that it spins round a full revolution. The 'Stamp' rule – when someone knocks his opponent's conker out of his hand – means he is allowed to stamp on his opponent's conker as long as he shouts 'stamp' first. (This rule can be harsh . . . but fun!)

It is possible to take a game too seriously!

Hiking
The Oldest Form of Therapy

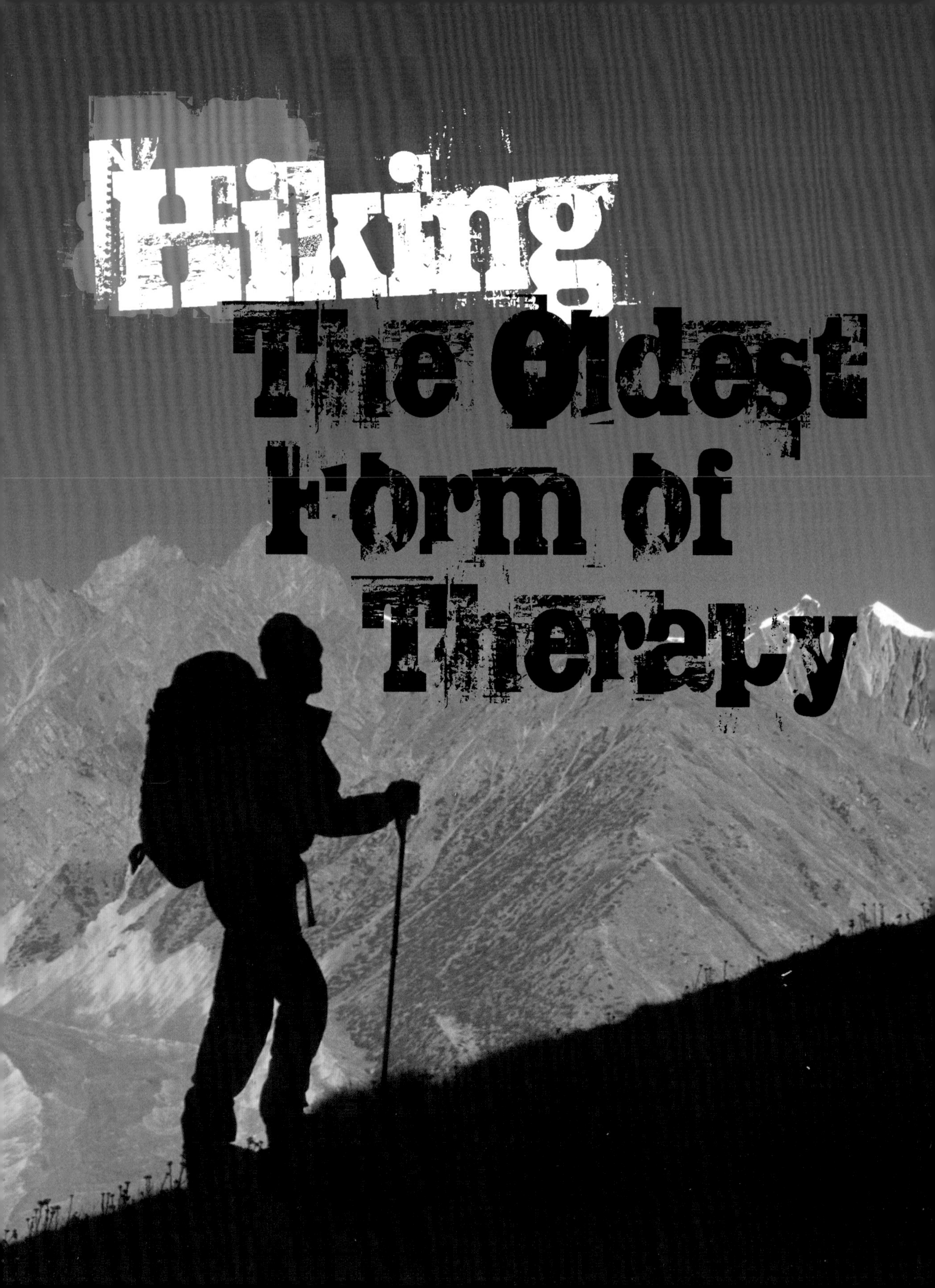

THERE IS SOMETHING profound about the ancient art of walking in the wilds. Whenever everything gets a little on top of me, when the fluff of life begins to weigh a little heavy, I know that a long hike in beautiful countryside will generally put things into a better perspective. Hiking is quite simply the oldest form of therapy known to man! Maybe that is why I love it so much.

You might have experienced the same feeling when you have needed to think through a problem or get over an upset in your life. Your first instinct is to go for a long walk. Well, scientists have now made a link between the rhythmical process of walking and the hypnotic steady rhythm needed for subconscious healing. In other words, the instinct to walk when seeking clarity or healing is scientifically proven to work. I love this fact.

It feels as if every step I take is a step towards a healthy mind. Each step is helping heal whatever it is in my life that needs some attention, and a little polish. A hike does me good mentally; it allows my mind to sift through the rubbish, tune up and stay positive. The blood moving around our bodies and brain, cleans the dirt, heals the cells, and unclutters the mind. Now that's good news, and might help you with your motivation the next time your buddy suggests a 20-miler rather than a 5-miler!

As a toddler my Dad refused to let me go around in a pram. So I toddled. And I toddled. And I learnt to walk long distances. Not much has changed really. The big lesson I had to re-learn though is that hiking doesn't have to be about pushing through pain barriers. So much of my military experience with the SAS was about huge hikes over many, many miles, day and night, through snow and blizzards, often on no sleep and limited food, at times being hunted by dogs and helicopters, and almost always carrying huge, heavy rucksacks. After a while I came to associate hiking with a painful experience that involved blood and blisters. (Despite that, I still somehow quite enjoyed it!)

Of course, it doesn't have to be that extreme. In fact the great pleasure for me now is to walk in the mountains with my family or good friends, take my time, rest when I am tired, have the odd sun nap in the heather, swim in a river en route, eat a picnic and bumble along peacefully soaking up the goodness that the natural world provides. (Man how things have changed, and boy does it feel good!)

Hiking really is one of the great bonding pastimes, whether you hike as a family with your kids on your shoulders (I've had plenty of that recently) or whether you are training hard in winter conditions over high mountains. The sheer process of humans moving steadily through rough country is as old as the hills you are walking in; and to share this sense of timelessness can be a very bonding experience. Along with fire and hunger, hiking is one of the few experiences that we have in common with our cavemen ancestors. And all it requires in the way of equipment is an inquisitive mind and a love of the outdoors. (Even having two legs isn't an essential; in fact one of the best hikers I know only has one of those!)

So have you got a good excuse to miss out on a pastime that can create bonds with your friends and family, brings good health to your body, unclutters your mind and allows you to immerse yourself in the great outdoors? In the same way that Bruce Lee called running the 'King of Exercise', I call hiking the cornerstone of all great outdoor pursuits.

Paragliding is much less fun unless you have earned the flight by a hike in; canoe trips don't quite have the same appeal without a hike out; and camping only becomes an adventure when it has taken you some foot time to reach the campsite. In other words: what you put in is what you get out. That's hiking for you.

Doing battle in the swamps of the Deep South in America. Less fun!

Every young hiker should have a good porter. (Dad!)

HIKING ESSENTIALS

It may seem obvious, but it never ceases to amaze me how many people I meet in the hills who have forgotten to bring basic equipment. Arming yourself with the essentials is easy and will add enormously to your enjoyment of the outdoors. There are lots of non-essentials (and I would usually include a GPS among them) that merely serve to make our packs heavier and our senses less aware.

But if you are planning hiking anywhere that is more than an hour's walk from a main road and on challenging terrain, keeping the following items with you will mean that you are very unlikely to come to any harm:

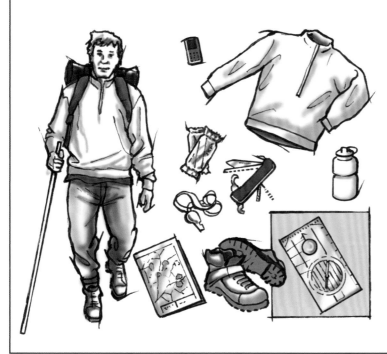

- Walking boots
- Waterproof (and preferably breathable) jacket and over-trousers
- Sun hat/sunscreen
- 1:50,000 (at least) map
- Pocket compass
- Water bottle
- Resealable plastic bags
- Spare energy bars – Kendal mint cake, etc.
- First aid kit
- Torch
- Knife
- Whistle
- Survival bag
- Mobile phone (in a freezer bag to waterproof it)

FIRST FOOTING

The history of walking is the history of our species. The very act of standing and walking on two feet is what first marked us out from the apes. And the footsteps of our ancestors, like a tantalizing telltale signature from the distant past, still echo down the long ages of our history.

Of all the countless footprints made throughout human evolution, almost all have disappeared. But two sets from opposite ends of the story still remain. The first sets were made in what is now Tanzania about 3.6 million years ago. They were made by three individuals, one of whom may have been a female carrying a child. By a near miraculous combination of an erupting volcano, baking sun, rain, and another fall of ash, the prints were preserved in almost pristine condition until the day they were discovered in 1976.

The second group of prints are on the moon. They were made on 20 July 1969, when Neil Armstrong became the first human to walk on

The ultimate step.

the moon famously saying as he did so, 'That's one small step for man, one giant leap for mankind.' Because the moon has no atmosphere, and therefore no wind or weather, the footprints made by Armstrong and Buzz Aldrin in the Sea of Tranquillity that day are more permanent than anything made by man that exists on earth and will last for millions of years. Just like the footprints of our distant ancestors in Africa, it's proof, if proof were needed, that walking is indeed the foundation of all man's great adventures.

HIMALAYAN TREKKING

If there can be said to be an 'original' adventure holiday, trekking must surely be it. Essentially the same as hiking or walking – 'tramping' as they call it in New Zealand – trekking means travelling by foot off the beaten track into mountainous terrain. This first became popular in the Himalayas in general and Nepal in particular in the 1960s.

The term itself was coined from an old Boer word meaning 'a journey by ox wagon' and the first Himalayan trekking agency, Mountain Travel, was the brainchild of an Englishman, Colonel Jimmy Roberts. A retired Ghurkha officer and mountaineer, Roberts was one of the first Westerners to explore Nepal, which remained closed until well after the end of the Second World War. Roberts ran his inaugural commercial trek in February 1965, recruiting the famous Sherpas of Everest fame as guides, cooks and porters.

The season for trekking in the Himalayas varies depending on geographical location and height. In Nepal the best trekking falls into two short bursts of activity, during March and April, and from September to November. After November everywhere above the snow line (about 3650 metres) is effectively cut off. During the summer the rivers are in flood from the monsoon rains, which spread north from the Bay of Bengal and hit eastern Nepal at the end of April. But between May and October the upper reaches of the Himalayan regions of India are passable. This includes areas such as Ladakh, Zanskar and the magnificent Spiti valley.

The mountains are timeless, that's why I love them . . .

. . . they also take your breath away.

The joys of trekking are self-evident to anyone who loves wilderness walking, but the experience is often as memorable for the unique cultures and peoples encountered in such remote places as for the inspiration of walking through sublime landscapes.

NORDIC WALKING

In recent years, a silent walking revolution spawned by the Scandinavians has been spreading across Europe. 'Skiing without snow' is how some people describe it and you'd be forgiven for thinking the same when you see a Nordic walker passing you in the hills in summer with not a snowflake in sight.

The Nordic Walking craze began in Finland when fitness instructors noticed how cross country skiers used ski poles while 'ski walking' and 'hill bounding' in the summer months to keep fit. The secret of its success as an effective route to fitness lies in the fact that the technique uses 90 per cent of the body's muscles – as opposed to 35 per cent when swimming and 70 per cent when running.

The arms are stretched while applying force to the poles, which in turn exercises almost all the muscles in the entire upper body. This improves aerobic endurance and takes the pressure off the hip, knee and ankle joints. The technique has been scientifically proven to improve fitness, reduce back and neck pain and increase strength, so it can't be a bad pastime!

Hiking in the Alps – hard work, but breathtaking (literally).

The French Foreign Legion added a new dimension to the word 'hiking'.

THE MUNRO BAGGERS

One of the most prized accolades for British hikers is to have 'compleated' – to use the traditional spelling – the 284 Scottish mountains known as the Munros. Named after Sir Hugh T. Munro, a Scottish laird and founding member of the Scottish Mountaineering Club (SMC), Munros are defined as mountain peaks over 915.4 metres (originally 3000 feet) and were first listed in 1891 when Munro's famous 'Tables' were first published.

While 'Munro bagging' – as summiting all the relevant peaks has become known – has been a popular pastime ever since, debate has continued to rage about what is, and what is not, a Munro. The first edition of the Tables lists 538 'tops' or peaks of sufficient height. These included peaks on ranges and ridges, but only 283 of these were judged by Sir Hugh to have 'sufficient separation' to be classed as mountains. It is the latter that came to be known as Munros.

When he died in 1919, Munro missed out on the hillwalking goal he inspired by the narrowest of margins, failing to climb two of his named peaks. The first 'compleatist' traditionally credited with climbing all the Munros was the Rev. Archibald Robertson in 1901. However, an entry in his diary recording the fact that he had to abandon one of his early climbs on Ben Wyvis has led some to question his achievement.

As the exact definition of a Munro is open to interpretation, and advances in surveying techniques have adjusted the official heights of many peaks, a definitive list has been hard to compile. However, the SMC, which adjudicates in such matters, currently states that there are 284 Munros, 511 'tops' and more than 4000 'compleatists'.

Munro himself missed out by the narrowest of margins.

LONG DISTANCE WALKING

Since 1965 when the Pennine Way in the UK was opened, twelve National Trails have been created across England, three more in Wales and four Long Distance Routes (LDRs) in Scotland – five if you include the northernmost six miles of the Pennine Way which crosses the border into Scotland. But these are by no means the only official long distance paths in Britain, of which there are well over fifty.

All the National Trails pass through National Parks, Areas of Outstanding Natural Beauty, and some of the most stunning landscapes in the country. All are well established and waymarked with the National Trails acorn symbol in England and Wales, and the LDR symbol of a thistle inside a hexagon in Scotland. Many people prefer not to attempt to walk the routes from beginning to end in one expedition but hike them a section at a time over several visits and sometimes over several years.

Picking out the best individual trails is almost impossible as they all pass through some of the most inspiring landscapes in Britain. Nonetheless, listed below are some of my personal favourites.

SOUTH WEST COAST PATH, ENGLAND

At 630 miles, the South West Coast Path is the longest footpath in Britain, running from Minehead in Somerset to Poole Harbour in Dorset. Along its route it takes in rugged cliffs, estuaries, harbours, moorlands, coastal valleys, coves and sweeping pebble and sand beaches.

Most walkers take between fifty and sixty days to walk the entire length of the path. During the walk it is estimated they will take around 26,500 steps while climbing and falling along the way, a combined altitude of 35,031 metres – almost four times the height of Mount Everest! (In fact, I did a lot of my Everest training here . . . and it paid off. 'Train hard, fight easy', as we were told in the army!)

The UK is blessed with some of the best coastal and mountain walks I know.

All that I love about the outdoors . . .

PEMBROKESHIRE COAST PATH, WALES

Wales's first long distance path follows the entire Pembrokeshire coastline. The scenery is wild and rugged with predominantly cliff-top paths with sweeping views over the surrounding cliffs, beaches and outlying islands. The path climbs and descends more than 10,660 metres over its whole length but also follows gentle shorelines, including the outer reaches of the Milford Haven estuary, one of the finest natural harbours in the world.

Of all the spectacular places I have been lucky enough to see around the world, the coast of Wales takes some beating. I consider Wales very much my spiritual home . . . the mountains, the sea and the rugged cliffs (oh, and no crocs or killer snakes in sight). It's heaven.

THE WEST HIGHLAND WAY, SCOTLAND

Scotland's most popular trail links its largest city, Glasgow, with its highest mountain, Ben Nevis, following the shores of its largest freshwater loch, Loch Lomond. It moves from the Lowlands across the Highland Boundary Fault and on into the Scottish Highlands. It was Scotland's first official long distance route and is now enjoyed by around 50,000 walkers every year.

THE RIGHT TO ROAM

The right to walk freely in the countryside is something that most of us take for granted. And so it should be. But the truth is that the right to wander at will in the wildest parts of the UK has been hard fought for. One of the most famous events in the long battle to preserve our wild places for everyone (and not just the big landowners) was the famous mass trespass on the moorland plateau of Kinder Scout, the highest point in the Peak District.

Sunday 24 April 1932 has long since entered into rambling mythology. At that time access to huge swathes of private land, including Kinder Scout (owned by the Duke of Devonshire), was denied to local people and a mass trespass of more than 400 people was organized to protest at this unsatisfactory state of affairs. On their way up to the plateau the trespassers came face-to-face with the Duke's gamekeepers and a scuffle ensued which the trespassers easily won. They then continued in a jovial atmosphere to the summit where they met up with a group of protesters from Sheffield.

Later that day, after they descended, the walkers were intercepted by the police and the 'ringleaders' arrested. Five of the men were jailed for between two and six months. It was a punishment that backfired badly though as public sympathy was firmly on the side of the trespassers, and the events of that day eventually led to the creation of our National Parks and the Access to the Countryside Act of 1949 whereby everyone is allowed access to public footpaths, regardless of whether they cross private land or not.

Despite this, huge tracts of moorland remained inaccessible to the public for another fifty years until the passing of the Countryside and Rights of Way (CROW) Act in 2000, and its final implementation in 2005.

WALKING WORDSMITHS

While people have been walking from A to B for thousands of years out of necessity, hiking in the hills for pleasure and as a tonic for the soul is a relatively recent phenomenon. And, perhaps unsurprisingly, it is one that has been celebrated by some of our greatest writers.

WILLIAM WORDSWORTH

Many of the Romantic poets were great walkers, and used the landscape as an inspiration for their work, often composing as they walked. The greatest hiker of them all was William Wordsworth whose experiences walking the Quantock Hills in Somerset and the Lake District fells he later immortalized in verse.

Wordsworth once climbed Snowdon at night to watch the sunrise from the summit and later braved revolutionary France for a walking tour with a friend from Cambridge. Wordsworth's passion for the hills never waned and in 1845, a full 15 years before his death, his friend the writer Thomas de Quincey estimated that Wordsworth had already notched up more than 180,000 miles during his walking life.

LAURIE LEE

Laurie Lee's justly famous and captivating book, *As I Walked Out One Midsummer Morning*, tells the story of his extraordinary adventures as a nineteen-year-old when he left the confines of his home, the Slad Valley near Stroud in Gloucestershire, to walk through central Spain on the eve of the Spanish Civil War.

Carrying just a rolled-up tent, some treacle biscuits and a violin, his account evokes the lost world of the hobo traveller in a simpler – if no less violent – world. The poverty of Spain's largely peasant society was no bar to the incredible generosity he received wherever he went.

ERIC NEWBY

Newby's eccentric classic, *A Short Walk in the Hindu Kush*, celebrates a uniquely British and happy-go-lucky approach to the joys of hiking in remote mountains. Newby describes how he and a friend travelled to the Nuristan Mountains of Afghanistan on a walk that turned out to be neither short, nor well planned. The author's comic, self-satirizing approach to the journey encapsulates a joyful and carefree approach to the possibilities of adventures on two feet.

Laurie Lee, author and great lover of the mountains.

ALFRED WAINWRIGHT

Wainwright's name is synonymous with the guides to the UK's Lake District and Scotland to which he gave his name, publishing more than forty books between 1952 and his death in 1991. The seven volumes of his *Pictorial Guide to the Lakeland Fells* were created over thirteen years and illustrated with Wainwright's trademark drawings. His no-nonsense style and passion for the subject have never gone out of fashion and his guides are currently in the process of being updated and republished for a new generation of walkers.

Wainwright is also famous for the English coast-to-coast walk he devised, taking in three National Parks – the Lake District, Yorkshire Dales and North York Moors – which runs from Robin Hood's Bay on the east coast to St Bees on the west coast. While the route is not recognized as one of the official National Trails, the thirteen-day walk remains one of the UK's favourite long distance walks.

PILGRIMS' PROGRESS

Walking as a path to spiritual enlightenment has been an important part of Christian tradition since Biblical times. One of the most famous pilgrimage trails is the Camino de Santiago de Compostela (also known as the Way of St James), which crosses northern Spain and is walked by tens of thousands of pilgrims every year. There is no single definitive route as pilgrims start the walk from a number of different points and today there are sixteen major paths. However, the vast majority follow the Camino Frances, which starts at several places in the French Pyrenees and follows back roads, footpaths and forest tracks along the way.

The pilgrimage ends at the cathedral in Santiago de Compostela in Galicia, where the remains of St James the Apostle are believed to be buried. Pilgrims queue to touch the cathedral's main pillar with their right hand. Over the centuries five distinct finger marks have been worn in the granite column. Pilgrims who have successfully completed the journey – 100 kilometres is the minimum acceptable distance – receive a 'compostela' or certificate of completion of the pilgrimage. This tradition dates back to medieval times when pilgrims would receive an 'indulgence' from the Pope to atone for their sins.

Walking isn't really going to atone for our sins, but it will make you feel a load better, and if you do a pilgrimage of this length you will also be a load lighter!

Pilgrims' reward: cathedral of Santiago de Compostela.

Navigation

Lost and Found in the Wild

Good navigating is about reading the landscape around you and looking for many small clues that confirm your position.

ONE OF THE fundamental skills you must learn in the wild is to navigate properly; it really is the key to accessing so many great adventures. Ultimately, however good you are at canoeing or climbing, it counts for very little if you are incapable of reaching the river or rock face unaided in the first place. I have lost count the number of times I have been out in the wilds and have had to use my navigating skills to search out a great hidden pool, waterfall or rock face that is off the beaten track.

The simple truth is that on this ever more crowded planet if you want to reach exquisite places and have them to yourself, you are going to have to navigate well to get there. Those great hidden locations are the good navigator's and hardened traveller's reward, and it is always worth it; in fact, it's half the magic.

I was in the middle of the Sumatran jungle and swampland recently, hemmed in on every side by the densest primary jungle you can imagine: deep gorges, massive gulleys, high ridges and jungle canopy, torrential rain, low visibility and slick mud everywhere. It was a nightmare to navigate in. We knew what we were looking for, but we had limited daylight to reach it. There wasn't time to get it wrong and the jungle is a very unforgiving place to be lost when it is that dense and vast. We had navigated most of the way, but the last leg was 500 metres in a straight line to a stream. In the jungle that sort of distance can literally take hours.

To follow a compass bearing in a straight line is not possible in these circumstances, as you are continually weaving in and out of trees, over roots and through undergrowth. I also knew that if we hit the stream 100 metres off target, it would be nigh on impossible to tell whether we were upstream or downstream of the location. So instead, we aimed our bearing intentionally off to the right, in order to hit the stream just north of our target. That meant that when we reached the stream we knew we had to turn left and follow it downstream until we reached our intended destination. It gave us room for the error that jungle movement forces on you. This was simple, smart navigation, and sure enough we hit it right. But such tips need to be learnt.

As we emerged from the undergrowth we saw this beautiful, hidden, translucent emerald green lake. Bigger than a tennis court, with crystal clear water running off a waterfall into the pool. It was pure magic. The pool had been an old volcanic vent and the calcium deposits deep down on the bottom kept the water a bright, clear green colour. It was clean and cool, and one of the most remarkable places I have seen. Like one of God's hidden gems, something you can imagine its Creator expected would never be found. A hidden extravagance of beauty amid one of the dirtiest, stinkiest, darkest jungles I have ever been in. You see: good navigation opens up wonderful worlds that without this skill you might never get to find.

Modern GPS is a great tool, but it is inherently flawed. Machines break down, especially electronics when it rains. And it is when it rains and visibility is low that you need the navigational help in the first place. I use GPS masses. It is amazing. But depend on it entirely at your own peril. It is a help but it is not a replacement for an age-old skill that man has honed over millennia. If you are into the outdoors, don't skip this chapter. It is vital. And the test always comes when you are alone, with no electronic aids and in a blizzard! Can you then find your way home?

Animals are the real masters of navigation; birds can migrate thousands of miles across oceans and deserts, in storms and fog and still locate the precise nest that they visit every year. Salmon return hundreds of miles upstream, through tributary after tributary, to the exact same spot they spawned. Instinct is a powerful tool, but for us humans that instinct needs to be learnt.

I have witnessed remarkable acts of navigation

Working our way through an icefall in the high Himalayas.

by men and women that without doubt have meant the difference between life and death for them. I remember waiting anxiously at base camp on Everest for two climbers to return after we had passed them descending the crevasse-ridden icefall. They were due back an hour after us. A storm had swept unexpectedly in, and six hours later there was still no sign.

The vast 900-metre ice labyrinth was now engulfed in deep powder snow, reducing visibility to nil and covering gaping crevasses in a deadly thin film of loose snow. By then it was also pitch black and the climbers had no head-torches. We ventured into the icefall to shout for them; we put up large spotlights to help guide them back

Mountains can be ruthless and turn against you fast. Be prepared, and plan for the worst.

if they were still alive. But the fact was that there was little we could really do beyond this. By heading deeper into this blind ice maze we were becoming as vulnerable as them.

The hours passed slowly, and each of those hours reduced the likelihood of the two climbers being alive. Eventually we heard muffled voices through the wind. The two climbers came stumbling towards us, shuffling steadily and together. They were frostbitten and exhausted, but alive. Their ability to navigate hundreds of metres off one of the most lethal ice faces on earth in that white-out, with no light, is a

Birds can migrate thousands of miles across oceans and deserts, in storms and fog and still locate the precise nest.

testament to their navigation skills. Had they been less experienced and not learnt the basics, they would still be in that ice labyrinth – dead.

BASIC SKILLS

Navigation is easy in good weather. But imagine a scenario like this. You are staying with some friends at a farmhouse on a moor. The visibility for miles around is excellent and your objective, a remote peak a few miles off, is beckoning benignly. Off you head straight towards it without a care in the world. The whitewashed farmhouse is shining like a sunlit beacon in the valley behind you and the water in the nearby lake is like glass with barely a ripple disturbing its placid surface. You'll be back in time for tea and crumpets, no problem.

Three hours later the hill seems no closer – in fact it's hidden behind an ominous-looking cloud – and the farmhouse has faded into the background and is barely visible now against the woods behind. The ground is beginning to get boggy underfoot. Somebody suggests looking at the map, except you don't have a map, or a compass and now a sleety rain is blowing against your face . . .

This sort of situation will be familiar to anyone who has ever allowed the impulse to dash off into an unknown landscape get the better of them. And a sudden change in the weather can render the most familiar scene unrecognizable.

Navigating is in fact very logical and can be both fun and easy to learn. In the end, it really comes down to three basic skills: knowing how to use a map; knowing how to use a compass; and knowing how to measure and judge distance over the ground. Never rely completely on hi-tech navigational instruments like a GPS until you have mastered the basics first. There is no better way of getting completely lost than being stranded without a map or a compass, blindly clutching an all-singing, all-dancing, 3D-technicolor GPS . . . that's on the blink!

MAP READING

Maps are amazing. With a map in your hand you are holding an exact replica of the world around you – but in symbolic form and on a minute scale. Learning to convert the information on this map into an accurate picture of the landscape in front of you is essentially what map reading is about.

Maps come in different scales; the most commonly used by walkers being 1:25,000 and 1:50,000. This means that one centimetre on the map is equivalent to 25,000 centimetres (250 metres) or 50,000 centimetres (500 metres) across the ground respectively. Different scales are useful in different circumstances. The 1:25,000 map gives more detail while the shapes of large features in the landscape like mountains and valleys are usually much clearer on the smaller 1:50,000 scale.

The first task of any navigational exercise – knowing where you are on the map – becomes much easier once you have orientated the map to the cardinal directions of the compass using the grid lines which run north/south and east/west. Once you have done that, you will be able to read off a grid reference to tell others your location, for example, or find a point on the map you want to reach.

The next task is to be able to accurately visualize and calculate height and distance from the symbols on the map. In your mind's eye you must learn to convert those squiggly contour lines into the shape of the hillside in front of you or the bottom of the valley behind you.

Knowing whether a hill is concave or convex can be very useful if you're deciding, for example, on the best route up it. Heights and distances to be covered can easily be calculated with a little practice and experience. Contour lines, usually in brown, join areas of equal height while the height

Accurate map reading takes practice. So practise!

The compass transformed man's ability to navigate simply (but you've got to know how to use it properly).

above sea level is listed at regular intervals. The height difference between contour lines on a 1:50,000-scale map, for example, is 10 metres. This would have been a useful thing to know when you were wondering how long it would take to get to the top of that hill and back again to your nice, warm farmhouse.

READING A COMPASS

Keep it simple. That's my best advice when it comes to choosing which compass to buy. The best ones for map reading come on a transparent base plate with markings around the outside, called a Romer scale, which are used for measuring off grid markings and distances on a map.

The primary role of the compass, however, is to tell you which direction is north. It does this when the strip of magnetized metal, which acts as a pointer, aligns itself with the earth's magnetic field. With this crucial piece of information, you will then be able to orientate the map correctly to the landscape and walk on a bearing.

In the event of being stuck on that hillside with the fog and the rain closing in, the combination of a map and a compass would have made it relatively easy to plot a course back to the farmhouse avoiding the lake and the marshy ground in between.

TIME AND DISTANCE – NAISMITH'S RULE

The final element in mastering the basic skills of navigation is to be able to convert the distance calculated from a map into the likely time it will take to cover that distance over the ground.

A useful rule of thumb was developed by the Scottish mountaineer William Naismith in 1892 and is still in use today. This assumes that a fit walker crossing even terrain in good weather will take an hour to cover 5 kilometres of ground and an extra half an hour for every 300 metres climbed.

In practice many people find it takes up to 50 per cent longer than Naismith's calculation especially when travelling in a group, so it's worthwhile noting how long it takes you personally to cover similar distances and making a mental note. Variables such as the fitness and experience of a group, the loads carried, the type and condition of the ground underfoot, and the weather conditions will all make a difference to the calculation.

During selection for the SAS we used to operate at about 4km an hour across high mountains, carrying heavy rucksacks, day and night, but this was always a fast pace to maintain. Whatever your pace is, take time to find out what speed you can maintain comfortably, and work to that. This knowledge will help judge your time and distances as you convert information from the map to the reality of the moor.

NAVIGATING BY THE STARS

The sun, the moon and the stars rise roughly in the east and move across the sky to set roughly in the west. This knowledge – combined with the observation of the North Star (Polaris) in the northern hemisphere and the Southern Cross in the southern hemisphere – was the basis of navigation for hundreds of years until the advent of the compass and reliable maps.

Navigating at night when you are lost without a map or compass, this basic knowledge can be the difference between life and death. At night, orientating yourself and following a fixed point that you know is not moving is vital. Most heavenly bodies are constantly moving across the sky.

In the northern hemisphere the exception to this rule is Polaris, aka the North or Pole Star, around which the constellations rotate. The best way to locate the North Star is to find the constellation of the Plough (aka the Big Dipper or Ursa Major), which looks like an old-fashioned ox-pulled plough or, more familiar in a domestic age, like a saucepan with a long handle. The two stars at the outer edge of the saucepan point directly at the North Star. Measure the distance between them in your mind's eye and then extend it outwards about four times. This will be the North Star.

In the southern hemisphere, look for the Southern Cross which, as its name implies, has a distinctive cross-like shape. Locate it by following the cloudy band of the Milky Way until you find a cloud of darkness like a blob of ink blacking out the sky. Near this blob of ink (known as the Coal Sack) is the Southern Cross. If the Southern Cross is upright, due south is directly below the central arm. If it's tilted, extend the central arm in a straight line towards the horizon by about five times its own length. Drop a plumb line from this point and you will be looking directly south.

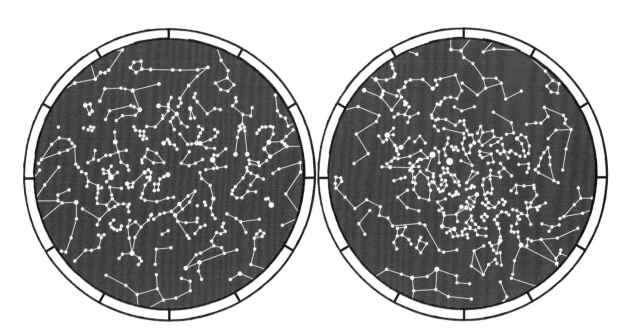

The North Star – the one constant in the northern hemisphere.

The Southern Cross – a very distinct marker in the southern hemisphere.

STAR SIGNS

On nights when the sky is partially obscured, pick any bright star and monitor its movement through the sky using two sticks set up like the sights of a gun barrel. In the northern hemisphere, the following can be deduced:

movement left: star is in the north
movement right: star is in the south
movement up: star is in the east
movement down: star is in the west
Reverse these rules in the southern hemisphere.

NAVIGATION BY NIGHT

Sometimes you will have no choice but to navigate by night. Maybe a hike has taken longer than expected because of injury or a miscalculation, or maybe you want to intentionally walk to a spot from where to get the best view of a lunar eclipse or the northern lights, or maybe you just want to get to a beautiful camping spot to watch the sunrise.

Whatever the reason, to the untrained, the dark night can be a daunting world to inhabit. But to those who can overcome that feeling of unfamiliarity, it can be a truly exciting space. The reason the night-time can seem so frightening and disorientating is that we are all used to depending on sight alone. But moving efficiently and confidently across mountains or wild backcountry in the dark requires you to use those other senses you possess but so often overlook, namely sound, smell and feel.

The common mistake that people make at night is to get 'spooked', and to start imagining features that aren't there. And when fear becomes your guide you make mistakes. You stop trusting your compass because you think you know better. That is a recipe for getting lost.

One of the first lessons we learnt with the Special Forces was how to move effectively at night. In fact, we would almost exclusively move at night; so night had to become our friend. But by summoning up a little confidence and adhering to a few simple skills, the ability to navigate well in the dark can be mastered and really enjoyed.

Navigating effectively without light requires the many skills of daytime navigation, but without the luxury of being able to correct errors visually. My mnemonic for a checklist for good navigational decisions is, 'Bear Drinks Tea For Breakfast'. This stands for Bearing, Distance, Time, Features, Backdrop. Mentally running through these before starting each leg of a journey is essential by day, but at night it becomes even more pertinent. By day, if you overshoot because you've been careless, it is easy to correct yourself if you can see the edge of the wood you were aiming for 200 metres to your right. Make this mistake at night and you could instantly be lost.

The accuracy with which you orientate and interpret your map in relation to features in the landscape will be the foundation stone from which everything else will follow. Your compass readings will need to be pinpoint accurate. And in poor visibility, when there is no moon or when a mist has come down, pacing and timing when you are walking on a bearing will be critical.

There are a number of good tips to be learnt; such as aiming your gaze slightly to the side of what you are looking at so you can see it more clearly. This is because the rods – which are far more sensitive to light although they cannot distinguish colour so well – are located in the outer part of the retina. And when you can't see features clearly, you need to recognize them differently: feeling when the ground underfoot is becoming softer and wetter; smelling a forest ahead; recognizing how shadow and depth of colour reflect off different mediums like woods, rocks or rivers.

Getting lost, even for a moment, will have far harsher consequences at night than in the day when a dominant feature in the distance may at least give you a point of reference. You need to be on the ball and to double-check and re-confirm every decision. But, with practice, being able to navigate confidently at night will open up a whole new world of adventure that remains closed to most people.

I have used this ability to operate at night many times in climbs and expeditions all over the world; from hiking through the African bush by moonlight to descending from a long route on a peak in the Himalayas during a white-out snowstorm. This skill has often come in useful at the most unexpected moments – but that's adventure for you, and the more of these skills you have in your armoury the better!

SURVIVAL NAVIGATION

Knowing how to work out the direction of the four cardinal points without a compass is a skill that everyone should take the trouble to learn. They are useful skills to have anyway and will improve your awareness and observation of what is going on in the landscape around you, but they could also be the difference between life and death. Knowing which direction is which in a featureless landscape like a desert is critical if you are to avoid going around in circles and using up precious supplies of energy and water.

SHADOW STICK METHOD

Find a straight stick about a metre long and as thick as your thumb. Break off any twigs and push it down vertically into some flat, soft ground. Carefully mark where the tip of the shadow falls and wait 15 minutes before marking the shadow tip again. The line between the two marks will be running approximately east/west. A line drawn at 90 degrees to this will be directly north/south.

The shadow stick method: to get rough cardinal points.

WRIST WATCH METHOD

In the northern hemisphere, point the hour hand at the sun. Then form an imaginary line between the hour hand and 12 o'clock. This is your north–south line. The height of the sun in the sky and the time of day will then show you which end of the line is north and which is south, remembering that the sun sets in the west and rises in the east. In the southern hemisphere, point the 12 o'clock mark at the sun and bisect that with the hour hand for the north–south line.

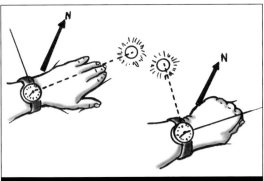

A watch and the sun: all you need to find north and south.

If you have a digital watch, just draw out a watch face in the ground with either the hour hand or 12 o'clock pointing at the sun, depending on which hemisphere you are in.

THE GPS REVOLUTION

The GPS or Global Positioning System is a navigational tool that can calculate the position of the user to within about 3 metres anywhere on the planet. It does this via a handset receiving signals sent out by more than 30 satellites orbiting the earth. These use atomic clocks to pinpoint the exact time when the message was sent out.

Depending on the position of the GPS on earth and the satellites in space, the receiver is able to receive signals from between about six and twelve satellites simultaneously, but only needs a minimum of four to generate an accurate fix. From the time delay of a few milliseconds from when the message was sent out to when it was received, the GPS is able to calculate the position of the satellite.

GPS – a fantastic tool but don't rely on it alone.

The position of the user is then calculated at lightning speed using complicated mathematics and the answer displayed on the screen. This includes the latitude, longitude, height and speed of the user, information that can also be displayed on a digital map. The GPS updates the user's position every second.

The system was developed by the US Department of Defense in the 1960s and 1970s to improve on the radio-based navigation systems used in the Second World War. These used radio waves transmitted from the ground but were not reliable or accurate enough for missile navigation. Following the shooting down of a Korean airliner that accidentally strayed into Soviet airspace in 1983, the GPS system was made available for worldwide civilian use. The system became fully operational in 1995.

While GPS can often be a very useful tool, it should not be relied upon in any but the most benign conditions. Wet, extreme cold and the general rough and tumble of wilderness locations are often too much for even the most robust unit. Sudden battery drain, especially in the cold, is also a common problem. Always have a conventional map and compass as backup and learn how to use them beforehand.

THE PUZZLE OF LONGITUDE

'How do you know you're lost if you don't know where you are?' is a conundrum man has been trying to work out since he first stood on two legs and began to wonder what was over the next horizon.

Navigation through landscapes with recognizable features such as rivers, hills or mountains was relatively easy. Distinctive points on the horizon could be used as a marker and followed for days at a time. At sea, navigation was more of a problem until man learned to use the stars to plot a course.

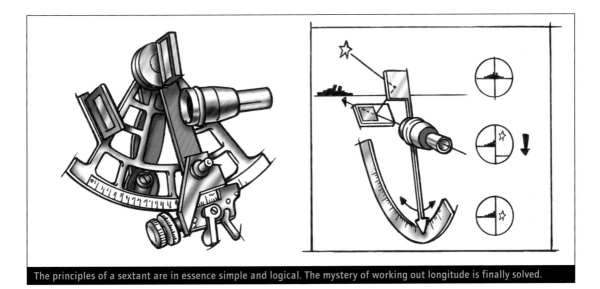

The principles of a sextant are in essence simple and logical. The mystery of working out longitude is finally solved.

The invention of first the compass and then the sextant – which measured the angle above the horizon of the sun, the moon and the stars with adjustable mirrors – meant that mariners could calculate their latitude (i.e. their distance north or south of the equator), but not their longitude. This meant that it was impossible for a ship to be sure of its exact position when approaching land, and many were wrecked as a result.

Following the loss of 1400 sailors off the Isles of Scilly in 1707 due to a navigational error, a large prize (worth more than a million pounds in today's money) was offered for anyone who could come up with a practical solution for determining longitude at sea.

At the time it was already understood that knowing the local times at two different points on earth could be used to calculate how far apart they were on an east/west axis (i.e. longitude). Calculating the local time by the sun was relatively easy. The problem was knowing the exact time at another known reference point.

The conundrum was eventually solved by a Yorkshireman named John Harrison, who was the first person to design a clock that remained accurate at sea, and which was later used by Captain Cook on his voyages of exploration. Claiming the prize, however, proved more difficult. Harrison's claim was not recognized until 1773, just three years before his death.

Better late than never!

Known as the H4, this was Harrison's first marine timekeeper.

Scrambling
A Real Sense of Freedom

LET ME START this chapter with a warning: scrambling is seriously good fun! While it is sometimes difficult to describe exactly what scrambling is, I have always thought of it as a way to enjoy hills and mountains without being restricted by anything except the most basic equipment. There will always be that grey area that divides scrambling from roped climbing, where on big routes the safeguard of a climbing rope is advisable, but what I want to convey here is the delight to be had from just scrambling up and over rocky terrain high in the mountains where there is little risk of a long fall.

This type of scrambling allows you to experiment; to run and jump, your mind and body absorbed in movement and improvisation as you clamber over and around huge boulders and rocks. For me it's pure escapism, a sport in which I can both lose myself and find myself. I can use all the dynamics of climbing. I can still scale a mountain, yet I can safely be unroped. That's the magic; you're not confined to a pitch or a route; it's just you, the rock and your imagination.

As a young kid, rocks and boulders felt like mountains to me, they gave me the chance to imagine I was on the highest peaks on earth. I used to scramble with my late father on mountains, sea cliffs and rock faces all over the place – even at home on the roofs and up along drainpipes! It was our best time together, just Dad and me, focused and free. We'd chat, play hide-and-seek among the rocks, or just sit and enjoy the views together. In this way scrambling gave me the first taste of the human bonds that climbing can create. I guess it is also where I found my intimacy with him, and that feeling of closeness has lasted all my life whenever I scramble.

But I also learnt then that in scrambling there are no restrictions; it is about using your

Scree running off the Patagonian steppe. Brilliant!

Brandberg Mountain, the highest mountain in Namibia, and from the top the desert looks amazing.

dynamic movement to overcome a rock face that from the bottom might look insurmountable. I had one of my best scrambling experiences recently in the middle of the Namibian desert on the way to the top of the Brandberg Mountain, Namibia's highest peak. From a distance the mountain seemed covered with small pebbles, but by the time I got to the foot of the face those pebbles had become rocks as big as houses. I soon found myself leaping over great drops between giant boulders and slithering in between cracks as I snaked my way up towards the summit.

Each new section of the scramble was a discovery; from finding beautiful hidden short chimney climbs to vast underground vaults beneath precariously perched giant rocks. It was like a thousand mini climbs in one day as I moved unhindered among rocks that most likely had never felt human feet on them. Moments like that are rare and, because I was unhindered by ropes and rucksacks, I felt as free as a bird.

Even to this day, whether filming the survival shows or on an expedition, like all of us I can have times when I am really struggling mentally, but if I start to climb freely, on my own, making my own instinctive decisions, my spirit will always pick up. It has happened to me many times, and because of this I associate scrambling with good things: being true to myself, being free, being good at something and being alive.

So the next time someone asks you what scrambling is, if you can't put it into words, take them out on a mountain and let them discover for themselves what is so hard actually to describe.

Let's have a stab at answering that question anyway. What exactly is scrambling? It's one of those questions to which nobody (even those who do it) ever seems to be able to give a precise answer. Everyone agrees that it lies 'somewhere between hiking and rock climbing', but where one of those activities ends and the other begins is a matter of some debate.

Everyone also agrees that the other key element in scrambling is using your hands to guide you on your journey forwards, sideways and upwards (and later downwards) on a rocky mountainside. Some say that to be a scramble rather than a climb, your hands should only be used for balance and not to hold your bodyweight; and that the maximum potential fall should always be less than 3 metres. According to this theory you will always be on terrain that is not so steep, exposed or uneven that you need to use climbing equipment like ropes, harnesses and pitons.

To make it even more confusing, 'roped scrambling' is something you will often read about in scrambling guidebooks, and surely if you're using ropes, then that's rock climbing? Well, yes . . . and perhaps no . . . it depends on how much you have to use them to get to the top in one piece.

There are arguments too about the way scrambling terrain is graded (see below). But the fact remains that the serious fun of scrambling is being out on the hills unencumbered by climbing

clobber and away from the boring predictability of a path that may also be crowded with other people. After all, apart from the serious Alpine and Himalayan peaks, you can normally reach the top of a mountain by scrambling up its least steep side. Scrambling is the equivalent of what skiers call going 'off-piste': leaving the safety of the path behind and finding your own unique route to the top of the mountain.

WHAT'S THE BUZZ?

Scrambling is all about freedom. The freedom to move unencumbered through a mountainous landscape using all your senses to their maximum potential. For most kids (and that includes me!), some form of scrambling is their first real adventure. Whether it's clambering over the rocks at the seaside or getting lost in the woods, nothing could compete with the thrill of getting off the beaten track and discovering that there's more to life than just following blindly where other people have been before.

Then there's the excitement, fear even, of the unknown; the discovery of a new way of experiencing the world (sometimes quite literally when you're halfway up a mountainside); the buzz of overcoming a physical challenge often in the most beautiful scenery; and – yes, you do need to be careful – enjoying that element of risk. After all, what's adrenalin for but to sharpen you up?

But it's the sense of achievement that makes it all worthwhile. Sure, the great peaks of the world are magical, but you can't climb them every day. And the real joy of scrambling is that you don't need any of the paraphernalia – rucksacks, ice axes, oxygen bottles, food and water – that are necessary on those kind of expeditions.

Basically, scrambling is almost like experiencing nature as the animals do, wild and unencumbered. And what could be more adventurous than that?

The serious fun of scrambling is being out on the hills unencumbered by climbing clobber.

CLASSIFICATION SYSTEMS

As with rock climbing, there are various classification systems used to describe scrambling routes based on technical difficulty, terrain and exposure to dangers like the weather or the risk of a dangerous fall. In the UK they are graded from 1 (Easy) to 3 (Difficult). In the US the Yosemite Decimal System (YDS) is used. YDS 1 is defined as General Hiking and YDS 5 is Climbing; scrambling routes are covered by YDS 2–4. Broad definitions are as follows:

GRADE 1 (UK)/YDS 2 (US)
EASY SCRAMBLING/ROUGH HIKE

Scrambling on uneven, exposed terrain in mountainous areas but with no major hazards and where route choice is not too difficult. You will need to use your hands to clamber over boulders and rocks and for balance from time to time, but ropes and technical climbing gear will not be necessary.

GRADE 2 (UK)/YDS 3 (US)
INTERMEDIATE SCRAMBLING

These scrambles will be on more difficult, exposed terrain with more challenging rock hazards and where route choice is more difficult and more committing. Hands will frequently be needed for small amounts of easy rock climbing but sections of vertical ascent will be short. A rope for emergencies should be carried as a fall could cause broken bones.

GRADE 3S (SERIOUS) (UK)/ YGS 4 (US)
DIFFICULT SCRAMBLING

These routes require a climber's knowledge of technical skills including the use of ropes and belaying. Although these skills may only be used

Scrambling only occasionally requires rope. In essence it is just you and the mountain.

in short bursts, the terrain will be exposed and route-finding challenging, especially in bad weather. Handholds will be in constant use and a fall could be fatal. Escape routes will be harder to find and may need to be abseiled.

A WORD OF WARNING. If you use a guidebook to decide on a particular scrambling route, it will have been graded for use in perfect conditions, when the rock is dry and not slippery. If the weather looks iffy or the forecast is bad, think of any route as a grade harder than described. Trust me, I have often been caught out. I was recently caught in a rainstorm up a rock face in the Black Hills of Dakota – it was like climbing on ball bearings!

THE SKILLS YOU NEED

Efficient movement over rock is something that improves with practice. Climbing is a natural instinct (just watch kids in a playground for a few minutes), but practice will improve vital skills like balance, rhythm and confidence.

You might think efficient use of your hands is the most important aspect of scrambling, but efficient use of your feet is far more important. The key is to maximize the contact between your feet and the rock at all times. Good footwork means that your whole body is stable and balanced from the bottom up. This will help to conserve energy and allows you to move to the next position in a flowing movement that will in turn allow you to build up the rhythm that inspires confidence.

Keep an eye on the clouds, rain can turn a perfect scrambling route into a nightmare.

It is important to keep at least three points of contact with the rock face at any one time. This means that your remaining free limb – whether it's a hand or a foot – can be used to explore your next position from a balanced position. Make sure it is solid and can take your full weight before you commit yourself to the next move.

I've often seen people who are new to scrambling or rock climbing using their hands to cling to a rock face when they would be far better advised to sort out their feet. Think about it like this; it doesn't matter how strong the walls of a house are, if the foundations are shallow or non-existent it will eventually collapse.

Another good tip is to try to keep your hands at shoulder height or below. If you raise them further up, the blood drains fast from your arms and fatigue comes on much sooner.

Scrambling heaven: the right rock in the right weather.

ON THE HILL

To be enjoyable and safe, scrambling requires the mind to be relaxed and in full control of the body. All five senses need to be in a state of calm red alert! Rhythm and balance are essential in your movements but also an awareness of what is above and below you, what is happening in the sky above, and how your scrambling buddies are getting along is also vital.

In some ways, the most exciting scrambles are those that take place on impulse, when the conditions are good enough to break away from the footpath or established trail onto broken terrain. On this type of outing, when a hike turns quite by chance into a scramble, you will still need to be wearing the right kit and be absolutely sure that the weather is set fair and the route to the summit is 'easy' scrambling terrain. When these conditions do apply, the sense of freedom can be very powerful.

Rock itself varies enormously and you should make yourself aware of its texture and feel right from the start. Is it secure? Will it take your weight? Is there a danger of rockfall from above or might you be sending rocks down onto someone below? Is it wet? Is it slippery? What type of rock is it?

And always let someone know that your plans have changed.

BASALT, FOR EXAMPLE – a type of volcanic rock – can be a nightmare when it's wet because it's so slippery. Gritstone on the other hand, which all scramblers love, is a sedimentary rock made up of the coarse sand and pebbles that once lined the seabed. It's what scramblers call 'well grippy' and feels really secure underfoot (although hard on the hands over time!).

By its very nature scrambling terrain is rough and it is up to you to work out the route you will be taking. Judging the suitability of the terrain and making the right choices is an important part of the skill of scrambling. It comes with practice and experience. But that's half the fun!

While getting into a rhythm as you move up a rock face or over a set of obstacles is all part of the thrill, always be aware of what is coming next. Objects look very different from far off than they do close-up and deciding your general route will be much easier if you've taken the opportunity to scan the terrain ahead in advance. If you scramble yourself into a cul-de-sac – particularly when it's exposed and there's a long drop below – you need to be absolutely sure you can make your way back to where the terrain is safer and reassess your choice of route. By studying the route in advance you will have a 'map' in your head of what to expect, and, even more importantly, what to be aware of on your way down.

JARGON BUSTER

OBJECTIVE HAZARDS

These are hazards that exist in the wilderness over which we have no control. They include: snow, ice, rain and all kinds of weather both hot and cold; falling rock; avalanche; altitude; sheer cliff edges . . . you get the picture. The best you can do is to try and overcome objective hazards with your skills and equipment, avoid them altogether, or minimize their effects.

Many mountains can be climbed from bottom to top by scrambling alone.

SUBJECTIVE HAZARDS

These are hazards that we can control but don't always do so successfully. Everyone has different levels of skill and experience, and it is this knowledge we use to make the judgements that keep us safe (or not) in the hills and mountains. Your knowledge can and will improve over time, but sometimes we are our own worst enemies, especially if we misjudge our own abilities. My advice on this is the same as the Ancient Greek philosophers: 'Know thyself' – be aware of your own limitations and stick to them.

GEARING UP

Good gear is important. It stops you getting into trouble in the first place, so it's worth investing in good quality kit and looking after it. Unless you are going to be scrambling on the most serious terrain, all you really need are standard mountain essentials, which include a good layering system of thermals to keep you warm, waterproofs, boots, gloves, some snacks and water and a map and compass.

Optional extras include a helmet, rope, harness and carabiners. But remember, these are just dead weight unless you know how to use them properly, so stick to easier scrambling routes until you do.

LAYERING AND WATERPROOFS

Keeping yourself warm and dry is the secret to any great day out on the hills. Layers of shirts and thermals are a great way of regulating temperature but remember you need to let the moisture from your sweat escape, so make sure your clothes are made of breathable materials – and take off layers before you start climbing. The aim is to avoid getting your clothes drenched in sweat, which will make you cold when you stop.

FOOTWEAR

The best footwear for scrambling is a pair of boots that are relatively light but have good sturdy soles. Try and use ones that have edges on the outside of the toe area that can support you safely and solidly when you stick your feet into rock edges or crevices. They also need to

The right kit, the right buddy, the right attitude – the key to staying safe in the mountains.

'Know thyself' – be aware of your own limitations and stick to them.

Climbing walls are the perfect way to increase strength and flexibility in preparation for the great outdoors.

support your ankles, which will be more prone to twisting and spraining on uneven terrain. Scrambling terrain is often wet, even if it's not raining, so waterproof boots will be a good investment.

HELMETS

Helmets are only really necessary if you're scrambling on terrain where there is a danger of loose rocks being knocked down on to your head from above. If you do need one, buy one of the modern lightweight versions made of Kevlar, polystyrene or carbon fibre rather than a traditional heavy climbing helmet. Make sure it fits and is adjusted properly. It mustn't be too tight on your temples (which will give you a headache!), but you don't want it falling down over your eyes during a delicate manoeuvre either.

So, scrambling is fun, but that very sense of freedom and being at one with nature can also make it potentially dangerous if you don't keep your wits about you. The very fact that you are at large in the hills without all the equipment required for technical rock climbing means that if you do get into trouble, it would be harder to get back to safety again without a serious mishap.

So, the first law of scrambling is to know your limits and don't get carried away. Beware of getting yourself into areas (an exposed ridge with a sharp drop-off for example) where a change in weather conditions or a gust of wind could make things dangerous.

The skill of scrambling is finding a satisfying route to the top across broken, mountainous terrain, but another part of that skill is not to be afraid to retreat and try a different route. Never commit to an upward move unless you know you can climb back down again to easier ground. Always be aware of exactly where you are on the mountain and the possible escape routes if something went wrong. Down climbing is a skill in itself and is often more difficult than climbing up. Remember, there are no safety nets in scrambling and you don't have to fall for it to be life-threatening.

As in all mountain activities, you should always let someone responsible know where you are going and when you expect to be back before you set out. Accidents, sadly, do happen and you may not be in a position to help yourself. Others knowing roughly where you are on the hill will increase the chances of a happy outcome considerably. And, unless you're very experienced, always go in a group. For a start it's more fun and you can look out for each other and give each other advice as you go. And stick together!

BEFORE YOU START

Scrambling is an extension of walking and is something most of us have done without really realizing there was a special name to describe it. But when you decide to take up scrambling as a serious outdoor pastime, it's worth preparing yourself well beforehand.

COURSES AND CLIMBING WALLS

Most outdoor centres offer courses in all types of outdoor activities and scrambling is now a recognized sport in its own right. On a weekend or five-day course, or even longer, you will be able to pick up the basics of the sport and get that invaluable hands-on advice from instructors who have had years of experience in the hills.

Climbing walls, which in the last few years have sprung up all over our towns and cities, are no longer used just by rock climbers and mountaineers. These days everybody's having a go and you should too. They will improve your confidence, flexibility and the strength of your muscles no end. They're also good places to practise the tricky – but essential – art of down climbing.

PLANNING A TRIP

If you plan to be scrambling on anything other than easy terrain, make sure you plan your trip well. Find out as much as you can about the route you're taking from guidebooks, the Internet or fellow scramblers who have already done it. The benefit of a local expert's knowledge can be invaluable in making the most of your day out.

Monitor the weather forecasts carefully for a few days before you trip. On the day itself, check the weather forecast again and make your own judgement based on what you can see in the sky before you set out. Bad weather will amplify hazards on a scrambling route and can turn even an easy scramble into a potentially dangerous one.

EARLY BIRDS

When you head for the hills, it's always worth getting an early start. Partly it's nice being ahead of any potential crowds on busy holiday weekends but it also gives you more time to sort out problems. On popular scrambling routes, it's also nice being above rather than below other scramblers, especially if there's a risk of rockfall. Oh . . . and if you are first up to the top you can have a doze in the heather before descending. It's a perfect day out!

Scrambling in the mountains of Kenya.

Foraging

Getting Food from Nature's Larder

MANY OF YOU reading this might think that I am the last person on the planet you should take advice from on the subject of finding delicious food! I do have to admit to the misfortune of having eaten some truly disgusting things over the years in the name of survival. But hey, this isn't a book about surviving life-threatening disasters; it is a book about how to have some great adventures outdoors, doing some wild activities and enjoying cosy times together with friends and family.

Now that is very different from eating yaks' eyeballs, goats' testicles, live snakes and giant scorpions . . . thank the Lord! So bear with me and let me take you on a bit of a whistle-stop tour of what nature has provided for us in the outdoors and what is often found in places you might never have thought of looking before.

You might be surprised to hear that I have a bit of a secret fear of lots of strangers in social settings; I find parties and receptions quite daunting. But give me a campfire under the stars with a few best buddies, some potatoes and wild garlic roasting in the embers, laughter, stories and songs and I am the happiest man in the world.

Why is it that simple food cooked on an open fire tastes better than any food in a fancy restaurant? One of the more memorable times of foraging and feasting I have ever had was with the San Bushmen in a very remote region of Namibia. We had spent the day tracking game together; but the way they track is not for any particular animal. Rather they wander around the bush foraging, looking for spore and fresh tracks, resting when the sun is too strong, and picking berries, herbs and leaves as they find them.

By mid-afternoon they had dug a large hare out from its burrow and this was now slung over one man's shoulders, and we each had an armful of nature's goodies in the form of wild potatoes, berries and herbal leaves. That night, with all the Bushwomen dancing around a fire that was spitting sparks high into the night sky while the men smoked their pipes, all of us tucked into a

Coconuts have been the salvation of many a desert island survivor.

Hunting is best learnt from those whose lives depend on it.

feast of flame-cooked hare in wild berries. What a privilege it was to have shared that time with these remarkable hunter-gatherers.

As I sat basking in the glow of the fire that night, I was reminded why the outdoors is so special. It levels people. It reminds us that man doesn't require fancy suits, smart cars or big TVs to be happy. A God-fashioned law of the universe is that happiness steals up on us in the least likely of places and rarely when we are busy trying to 'get' stuff that we think will 'make' us happy. Instead, it is much more likely to be found when we stop, sit still with good friends in nature's garden and listen. I remember something my grandfather used to say: 'There is always music in the garden, but our hearts must be very still to hear it.' Add to this some wonderful food that you have found, prepared and cooked yourself over a fire, and you know what? I bet a feeling of happiness and wellbeing will have quietly crept up on you, too.

FOOD FOR FREE

For our hunter-gatherer ancestors an intimate connection with the land and the seasons was a necessity. Foraging for food was as natural to

them as sleeping or breathing is to us and it is one of the oldest, if not the oldest, outdoor activity known to man.

Today it is all too easy to take food for granted. Supermarkets and fast food outlets have so perfected the devilish arts of convenience that many kids have no idea where their food actually comes from. Taste and texture have been sacrificed on the altar of uniform shape and the 'perfect' colour. With them have gone much of our sense of connection with the land, the rhythms of the seasons, and our knowledge of which of nature's many foods are good to eat.

In truth, free food is all around us, even in the wilder spaces of our cities, if we have the eyes to see it and the desire to find it. Almost all the vegetables we see in the shops had a wild ancestor

And you can never start to learn such skills too young!

and many have folk names associated with them – 'penny bun' and 'horn of plenty' mushrooms, for example – which give potent clues as to their appearance and edibility.

But thankfully, alongside the rise of organic food and the 'slow food' movement, there has been a reaction against the 'time is money' world of speed and convenience. More and more people are enjoying the simple pleasures of foraging for food, which can often be a lot more nutritious and tasty (not to say cheaper) than anything available in the supermarkets.

HEDGEROW SUPERFOODS

These days the health pages of our newspapers and magazines are awash with articles about the health-giving properties of the latest 'superfoods' stuffed with vitamins and nutrients to keep us young and healthy forever. But, perhaps unsurprisingly, they often come with a healthy price tag attached.

However, if health is the aim, we need look no further than our hedgerows to find foods stuffed full of the same vitamins, nutrients, and minerals as their more glamorous cousins and just as effective at combating life-threatening diseases like cancer and heart disease.

Wild foods, by definition, have not been processed or tampered with in any way and have been shown in studies to be far more nutritious than cultivated foods. They are often full of dietary fibre which is good for our guts; vitamin A (good for the skin and eyes and for fighting infection); vitamin C (an antioxidant that the body does not produce itself and excellent for fighting disease) and Omega-3 fatty acids, found in fish, which lowers blood pressure and is good for the heart.

And there are two hedgerow foods that can be found during most of the year which are particularly nutritious, but which are often seen as just rank weeds. So while nettle soup or dandelion salad may not sound as exotic as royal jelly, it's certainly a lot cheaper and harvesting them yourself is half the fun.

NETTLES

I've never met anyone who can't recognize a nettle. And if you've never been stung by one, well this book's probably not for you. Incidentally, those painful shots of formic acid and histamine will have done your immune system a power of good.

Even so no one actually likes getting stung, so arm yourself with a thick pair of gloves that cover your wrists when you pick them. The small leaves

Nettles: painful but one of the healthiest foods around.

at the very top of the plant are best (and at their freshest in early spring). They can be mashed up into soup and also make a good spinach substitute. The sting disappears when the leaves are dried or cooked and they are full of vitamins A and C, minerals (especially iron) and have a very high protein content. Other life-enhancing ingredients include calcium, magnesium, iodine, serotonin and amino acids. Nutrition doesn't get much better than that. Nettles also purify the blood and, if granddad's getting a bit old and creaky, they're said to be great for arthritis.

DANDELIONS

Dandelion leaves have been famous for their medicinal qualities for centuries. Back in the days when poets all died of 'consumption' (or tuberculosis as it's now known), the healers of the day prescribed dandelion leaves in spring and their roots in winter.

This habit was not without good reason. Dandelion roots, which gardeners are so keen to dig up and which can sometimes penetrate more than 45 centimetres into the ground, suck up goodness aplenty. Their leaves are chock full of vitamin A, potassium, iron and lecithin (which helps keeps cholesterol at bay). They make an excellent tonic for the liver and the kidneys.

Dandelions: beautiful and another of the healthiest foods.

To avoid the bitter taste, which comes on in summer, pick the youngest winter or spring leaves from plants without flowers. They are delicious in salads and taste like chicory and endive.

EAT YOUR GREENS!

The green leaves of edible wayside plants are both easy to find and often the most nutritious. Of all foods, they are the richest in vitamins and minerals. They cleanse the gut of mucous and toxins and help produce haemoglobin which carries oxygen

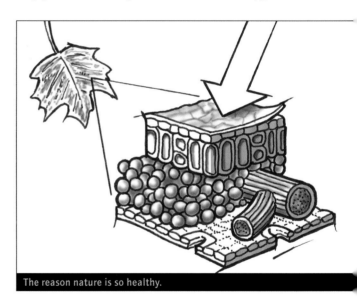
The reason nature is so healthy.

around the body. In fact the very reason these foods are green is because the chemical that makes them green – chlorophyll – is one of the most important building blocks of life on earth. This is what traps the energy in the sun's rays to convert to glucose, which animals (and humans) can then later convert back into energy.

About a quarter of the weight of wild leaves is protein and they are also full of dietary fibre, which for many people is less of an irritant to the gut than other more popular sources like the wheat we get in our cereals.

SORREL

This is one of the most recognizable of wild foods. Its tiny flower heads, on their long stalk, turn from green through orange and rust red to brown during May, June and July. Its long, thin, pointed leaves look like the business end of an African hunting spear. Lemony sorrel leaves are among the tastiest of wild foods, and can be eaten raw in salads or made into a delicious soup. Identification is made easier by the distinct arrowhead shape at the bottom of the leaf. Early spring is the best time to pick them, as they tend to develop a sour taste later in the summer.

Sorrel adds a delicious lemon flavour to salads in early spring.

WILD GARLIC

Wild garlic is a very common plant in damp woodland and hedges from March onwards. Its pungent smell is usually the big giveaway but you can recognize it later in the summer from its white star-shaped flower and its broad, pointed leaves. The taste of the leaves is not as overpowering as you might think and they taste great in salads or as a snack when you're strolling in woodland. The flowers are also edible but have a stronger taste. Like cultivated garlic, it's also very good for you, reducing cholesterol and high blood pressure.

Garlic: delicious but bad for your camping partner!

CHICKWEED

The great thing about chickweed is that you can find it at almost any time of year and it is actually tastiest in autumn and winter. The leaves are small and soft and are best plucked in handfuls as they are really too small to be picked individually. The stems can be eaten as well. Best eaten in salad. Cooking tends to break it down into a tasteless mush.

ALEXANDERS

Alexanders are a bit of an acquired taste but are a common hedgerow plant, especially near

Alexanders: out of fashion now, but still a tasty herb.

the sea. The plant was first brought to the UK by the Romans who used it as a herb. The leaves taste a bit like celery and the solid hairless stem can be boiled and eaten like asparagus.

SEAWEEDS

People have foraged for and eaten seaweed since prehistoric times and some varieties are still considered delicacies in many countries around the world. In ancient Chinese histories, seaweed is often described as a delicacy fit for a king and in the Far East today, particularly in Japan, more than twenty species are used in everyday cooking.

There are said to be as many as forty edible species of seaweed around the coast of the UK today, but the definition of the word 'edible' can sometimes be open to question. Just because it's not poisonous doesn't necessarily mean it makes a great culinary experience.

Seaweeds are known for their nutritious qualities and are rich in minerals. Like flowers, seaweed grows in the summer and dies back in winter and is best harvested in spring and early summer. When foraging for seaweed, make sure you cut it well below the anchor point on the rock so that it can grow back again.

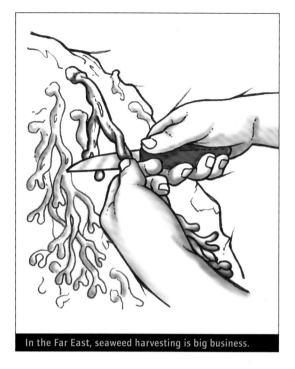
In the Far East, seaweed harvesting is big business.

SEA LETTUCE

Like all green seaweeds, sea lettuce likes shallower water. It looks a bit like the cultivated variety and can be eaten raw. It tends to grow in estuaries where freshwater rivers run into the sea.

Sea lettuce is harvested in shallow water.

One of nature's richest sources of goodness.

POPWEED (BLADDER WRACK)

One of the most common seaweeds, popweed is easily recognized by its distinctive air-filled blisters. It's very likely that you will find the kids popping the blisters on the beach. It should be boiled gently and served as a vegetable.

Popweed: delicious boiled and served with butter.

PURPLE LAVER

This variety of seaweed is popular in Wales where it can be bought as laverbread puree (and eaten for breakfast). The laver's shiny deep purple fronds are easy to recognize and are found on rocks, mainly on the Atlantic coast, after the tide has gone out. It is very nutritious and full of protein, carbohydrate, vitamins and iodine.

CARRAGHEEN

Popularly known as Irish Moss, this purple-brown weed, with its flat branching fronds that look like spanner heads, is often used to thicken stews, in jellies, ice cream or even as sausage skins. It prefers warmer, more southerly Atlantic shores and is very common in the Channel Islands.

MUSHROOMS

Mushrooms and other fungi can be foraged year-round, although they are most abundant in autumn and are one of the most popular and tasty wild foods. There's just one problem. While there are more than a hundred edible species in the UK alone, they are also very easy to misidentify. The result can be a bad case of the runs at best, or a permanent berth in the local cemetery at worst!

So always go foraging for mushrooms with someone who knows what they are doing and always take a well-illustrated field guide, which will have detailed illustrations, photographs and descriptions (and often a skull and crossbones beside the more deadly varieties).

A good tip is to learn the deadly mushroom varieties and avoid them – and any similar-looking mushrooms – like the plague. Also, remember that mushrooms should only be picked when they are dry and with no sign of decay. That said, nothing quite beats spending a warm autumn day in the woods and meadows helping yourself to a delicious meal from nature's table.

The wild mushrooms listed opposite are some of the tastiest (and most easily recognizable) varieties.

Poisonous fly agaric mushrooms – avoid them.

ST GEORGE'S MUSHROOM

These are easy to identify as they are the only large, white mushrooms that pop up in spring (around mid-April). They usually have a creamy tinge with a darker section towards the middle and dense white gills on the underside. They have a firm texture and a very pungent taste like woodsmoke. They are often found on chalky downland.

St George's: firm texture, meat-smell, distinctive flavour.

PARASOL MUSHROOM

Now, these I especially love! They are so called because they look like a lady's parasol and are usually to be found in meadows so you can often spot them from quite a way. The scaly cap is egg-

Parasols: strong flavour, excellent for pickling and freezing.

shaped to start off with and later breaks out into the flat shape from which they get their name with a leathery dark brown section in the middle.

SHAGGY INK CAP

This is another distinctively shaped variety of mushroom, with a preference for meadows and roadsides. They look like white versions of the bearskins worn by the guards outside Buckingham Palace. They are best picked when the cap is still closed. They taste a bit like shellfish.

Shaggy ink caps: lovely sliced and fried for breakfast.

CEP

These are another top find. Ceps are absolutely delicious and are often called 'penny buns' as the cap looks like the glossy brown surface of a currant bun. The gills are very distinctive as they look like tightly packed spongy tubes.

Trees are one of the best resources you can use for adventure, survival and food.

Blackberries. Yum yum, my favourite!

GIANT PUFFBALL

If any mushroom looks like it will be poisonous, it's a giant puffball. In fact, they are one of the most delicious of all foraged foods. You usually find them by mistake and some are as big as a football and look like an ostrich or dinosaur egg. Great!

FRUITS

The reason wild fruit is so bursting with sweetness is actually a cunning ploy on the part of Mother Earth as they are the only one of nature's foods whose specific purpose is to be eaten. Our job – or more often the birds – is to spread their seeds far and wide after they have been in at one end and out the other.

Wild fruits are high in antioxidants, which help keep cancer at bay, and the smaller, wild berries that are the genetic ancestors of the cultivated varieties – strawberries, raspberries and gooseberries are all good examples – have much more goodness in them pound for pound than the shop-bought varieties. The berries mentioned above (along with blackberries, of course) may be the most popular wild berries, but don't miss out on these two less common varieties.

ROSEHIPS

Rosehips have about twenty times the vitamin C content of oranges and are also a good source of vitamin A. They make a great tea if steeped in

Rosehips are high in vitamins A and C.

boiling water but can also be minced up into a delicious and nutritious syrup. The main problem with rosehips is that they are fiddly to pick and the hairy seeds can occasionally irritate the stomach.

BILBERRIES

Bilberries can be difficult to find as they like windswept moorland in northerly latitudes (think Canada, Wales, Scotland and Norway). But if you are lucky enough to find a source of wild bilberries, don't pass up the opportunity to pick some. They make delicious jam and are awesome in cheesecake!

Bilberries: the wild variety of blueberries.

NUTS

Autumn, as the poet Keats reminded us, is a time of 'mellow fruitfulness' and – as any squirrel will tell you – nuts are one of its most potent blessings. Nuts make a great foraging food, but remember that many woodland animals depend on nuts for their survival over the coming winter, so go easy, and share!

HAZELNUTS

As any chocoholic will tell you, hazelnuts make a great ingredient in chocolate bars but they also make a tasty snack to munch on an autumn walk and can be grated up and added to a leaf salad. Or why not try a hazelnut cutlet which is stuffed full of protein and carbohydrates. They are best foraged around mid-September.

Hazelnuts are a delicious part of the September harvest.

SWEET CHESTNUTS

I'm a sucker for a bag of chestnuts when I smell them being roasted over a brazier at the onset of winter, but how much nicer to find them yourself on a walk in the country and to roast them in

Roasting chestnuts is a sure sign that Christmas is near.

the ashes of a fire when you get home. Here's a tip: slit the skins and put them in hot ashes but leave the skin of one untouched. When that one explodes, the rest will be ready to eat.

FLOWERS

Eating flowers is not something most people would consider. But, then again, most people don't have much fun! Flowers can actually be very tasty and nutritious, with yellow flowers in particular being a good source of vitamin A. The flavour and texture of flowers vary from species to species, but it's not just the petals you should be eating. The pollen and nectar so sought after by insects can make them deliciously sweet. Some are very crisp and crunchy while others are almost silky soft.

ELDER

While most people associate elder with its berries, which make great wine, its flowers can also be made into a delicious cordial and have traditionally been used in any number of medicines and ointments. The flowers can also be added to salads to liven things up, or just munch them straight off the tree. (Best way yet!)

WILD ROSE

Wild rose petals can be eaten raw, but are usually made into jams or included to spice up other foods, such as adding a touch of summer fragrance to salads, honey or jelly. They are best picked in high summer just before they drop off the bush.

Elderberry flowers are much underrated.

Wild rose petals are best picked in high summer.

Making Yours
in the Great

10

Camp Building

Yourself at Home Outdoors

CAMP BUILDING AND camping out are pastimes that keep you young at heart and grateful to be alive. They also keep you appreciating home, when you eventually make it back, all too often soaking wet and muddy!

The two main things I have learnt over the years about camps are first of all that time spent carefully building your 'home' is rarely wasted, and secondly to build your camp before it's dark!

I remember one of my earliest camping trips to the mountains in North Wales. I was 13 and was with Watty, one of my best buddies. It was early evening and finally we arrived at the base of the mountain where we were going to camp. While everyone else carefully put up their tents, we messed about wading in a stream and lobbing rocks into deep pools. By the time we came to pitch our tent it was dark and we did it hurriedly in an effort to get on with the more serious business of supper and stories round the fire.

Later, when we eventually crawled into our sleeping bags, the weather was worsening. By 2 a.m. we were in a gale. We buried ourselves deeper into our sleeping bags and tried to shut out the wind and cold and rain, and prayed the tent would hold out.

It didn't! At 3 a.m. both A-frame connectors snapped. Minutes later we were rolling around in the dark, amid a jumble of string and canvas. We tried frantically to repair the tent but were soon soaking wet, freezing cold, and covered from head to toe in mud. The rest of the night was

They say necessity is the mother of invention. Ask the Mongolians who live and survive at minus 40 degrees.

Building camp is always fun, although less so in an alligator-infested swamp.

spent huddled up in a ball, shivering and truly miserable!

Since then, however tired I am at the end of a day's hike, when it comes to setting up camp – whether it's a tent, a bivvi or a shelter – I take my time and do the job properly. My mum used to say, 'When a job is once begun, leave it not till it is done; be it big or be it small, do it well or not at all'. Rarely can a phrase so aptly apply as this does to camp building.

I went camping with friends in Australia recently. Sure enough, as evening fell they all pulled my leg as I carefully set up my poncho and hammock while they sat round the fire drinking. By the time we all turned in the sky was crystal clear, not a cloud in sight. Most of the guys didn't bother with their tents, they just threw a roll mat and sleeping bag down and crashed out. By 3

a.m. we were in one of the heaviest downpours I have ever witnessed anywhere!

Everyone was running around like headless chickens trying to find tents in the dark and shouting to each other over the noise of the rain. Even though I got soaked helping them out, I did also feel a twang of satisfaction that I had been proved right! A lot can happen to the weather during the night, so be prepared. A few well thought out minutes before you go to sleep is always better than a night in the drink! Indeed, the Army drilled into us this discipline of tending to your shelter, weapon and feet properly before you collapsed at the end of a day.

But so far I have painted the darker side of camping and camp building. I promise the upside is much greater! It's the simple pleasure of making a small patch of the great outdoors your very own

home, safe from predators and weather; it's sharing a camp with close friends or family and telling stories late into the night under a patchwork sky of stars, until you all fall asleep without knowing it. Indeed sleeping out is one of the fundamental joys necessary to experience life to the max.

It reminds us that the best things in life are free – laughter, fresh air, watching nature's TV (a good fire!), close friends, camp food, shooting stars, tall stories and squinting at the mountains on the moon. It doesn't get much better than that.

The list of places I have slept out is quite long now, whether it's been high up trees, under huge rocks, on narrow mountain ledges or inside animal carcasses! But, for what it's worth, if I had to list my top three camps ever, they would be, first, the South Col on Everest, at 8848 metres. Not for the pleasure value but the life moment value. It was minus 45 degrees in a

howling gale and we were two very scared men huddled close for warmth. Second would be in the jungles of Central America in a tropical thunderstorm where the ground around us was literally shaking with the proximity of the lightning cracks. And lastly, it would be camping near home with my wife and two young boys, 200 metres from our house, tent full of duvets and home-comforts, with the closest thing to proper camping equipment being an old guitar. Heaven!

In fact it is worth saying again: the best things in life really are free. So go and make a camp. And, as a little postscript to this chapter there's a piece on camping in a cave. My five-year-old son always quotes me a line from his favourite bedtime story, 'Be strong, be brave, you haven't slept out 'til you've slept in a cave.' So, give that one a go as well. They can be awesome!

CAMPCRAFT

There's a right way and a wrong way of doing everything in the outdoors. And that's not because of some dusty old rulebook made up by a schoolteacher. All these techniques have been worked out the painful way – by trial and error in the field – before a general agreement about which way works best has been reached. It will usually be just plain common sense, but that common sense is never obvious the first time you find yourself in a new situation and are tired, cold and wet. Which is why it's always worth learning a few golden rules beforehand.

These techniques have been worked out the painful way.

GOLDEN RULES OF CAMPING

Make sure you arrive at the site where you plan to spend the night well before nightfall. Making camp in the dark, let alone the wind and the rain, is a recipe for disaster. Flat, soft, earthy ground is best both for comfort and into which to sink tent-pegs. Think about where your tents or shelters, cooking, eating and loo areas are to be located and keep them well apart from one another. Your sleeping quarters should be upwind of the fire and, if possible, sheltered by a windbreak. If you are near water, check the campground won't be flooded in the night, and if there is any doubt, find higher ground. Dig a drainage ditch around your tent or shelter if a thunderstorm looks likely.

Nights spent in the wild (even in a lightning storm) are life-enhancing moments.

One of the tougher places I have ever camped and survived – the South Col on Everest at 8000 metres, entering the 'death zone'.

TENTS

Choosing a tent can be a difficult task. But, as with all decisions about equipment, ask yourself some key questions before you buy it and you're more likely to make the right decision. What type of camping do you have in mind? Are you planning on taking it with you on a backpacking

it's pitched before you make your decision.

There are many different types of tent ranging from the old-style ridge tent with a rigid pole assembly, through to modern geodesic dome tents and lightweight tunnel tents. Dome tents can be pitched without guy ropes and perform well in high winds, while tunnel tents are small and lightweight and popular with backpackers.

Even without a tent, a fire makes a camp feel more like home.

trip or will the whole family be using it on summer weekends by the coast? Will you be using it in testing wilderness conditions? Will you be continually moving or establishing a base camp? Will it be a home-from-home or an overnight bivouac before moving on?

Annoyingly, you may well find the answer is yes to all of these questions, in which case you need more than one tent! But at least you then won't fall between two stools and get a tent that doesn't do the job well in any of the scenarios you have planned. Try and see what your tent looks like when

You can also get self-erecting tents that just 'pop' up automatically, although in my experience of testing these on mountains in gales they are fast to put up but a nightmare to try to repack. I also love the 'yurt' type of tents, that are traditional style, heavy duty canvas, and once properly pitched will endure the toughest conditions and can be kept warm with a small stove inside. But these are for more longer-term trips.

The most important consideration is to balance the weight and size of the tent with its likely performance when the going gets tough.

SLEEPING BAGS

Whether or not you stay warm and dry is the difference between heaven and hell on a camping holiday. Listening to the drumming of rain on canvas may not be what you originally had in mind, but it can actually be a great cosy experience if your kit is up to the task. I love the sound of rain when I am dry!

While the essential task of a tent is to keep you dry, the essential task of a sleeping bag is to keep you warm (but not too warm!) and also to be the right size and weight to make carrying it an easy task. So when you're choosing a sleeping bag, keep in mind the following things. Sleeping bags keep you warm by trapping the warm air generated by your body in the filling. These are either natural fillings (down and feather) or man-made synthetic materials. There are advantages and disadvantages to each. Down, the softer under-plumage of ducks and geese, is light and a fantastic insulator but loses its warmth instantly when wet and can take an age to dry out. Modern synthetic fillings, on the other hand, resist water, dry out quickly, and are warm even when damp, but generally don't compress down as small. This is where the construction of the bag – how it is

Dawn from a tent shared with good friends is always a wonderful sight.

shaped, stitched and quilted – will be critical as the efficiency of its heat retention will dictate how big or small it will be.

Sleeping bags are generally categorized as two-, three-, or four-season bags, depending on their ability to retain heat. But remember a four-season bag may keep you warm in temperatures well below zero, but it will also be unbearably hot in summer. Most manufacturers provide a temperature rating that will tell you the range of temperatures at which a healthy adult can expect a comfortable night's sleep.

SURVIVAL SHELTERS

Survival shelters can save your life when you're stranded in a jungle or halfway up a mountain in a rainstorm, but they can also be great fun to build when you're hiking in the hills and forests and want to practise your wilderness bushcraft skills. The type of shelter you build will depend on the type of terrain and the weather conditions. If you are smart you will aim to try out your first survival shelters in the summer when the nights are warmer (if not necessarily drier), and will choose a location like a wooded area where there's a ready supply of wood and undergrowth.

Never start building until you've had a good look round to make sure you've chosen the best possible location. Nothing is worse than discovering as night begins to fall that your lovingly constructed shelter is actually in a gulley that will flood the moment it starts to rain. Higher ground will also often be a few degrees warmer than on a valley floor. (Placing your shelter just 25 metres above the valley bottom can make a significant difference in avoiding the cold air that sinks to the valley floor at night.) Build at right angles to the wind so your shelter doesn't become a wind tunnel. Think of positioning the entrance facing east so you catch the first rays of the sun in the morning.

TRIPOD DEBRIS SHELTER

The trunk of a tree makes an excellent foundation pole around which to build tripod-shaped structures. Choose a tree that is smooth, straight and free of low branches and no more than about

Tripod shelters

half a metre in diameter. Then gather as many dead branches as you can find and build a tripod shape around the trunk with an entrance at the front. Now gather some smaller twigs and saplings and 'thatch' them crossways so the structure is strengthened before piling on debris in the form of foliage and bracken to cover the whole structure.

BENDER

Young saplings can sometimes be found growing together in such a way that bending them towards each other and lashing them at the top will make a structure much like a dome tent. If they are not conveniently placed, cut some down, dig a series of small holes in a circle and push the saplings into the ground before lashing their tops together as above. Weave branches and foliage into the structure to insulate.

A-FRAMES

Find a strong, straight branch and lash each end to two further pairs of poles in an inverted V-

Bender shelter

shape at either end. Decide which end will be your door and weave a grid of branches and foliage for the walls and the back of the structure. Then 'thatch' with saplings and cover with leaves and foliage as for the debris shelter.

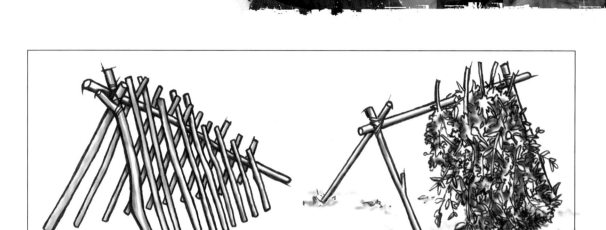

A-frames

The A-frame concept can also be used to make a raised bed that will keep you clear of the cold ground and away from any bugs and creepy crawlies that may be eyeing you up for a good feed. Lash together two sets of poles into inverted V shapes as before. Then tie two bed-length poles lengthways between the inverted Vs and halfway up them. Weave a strong mesh webbing of plant material between two poles like a hospital stretcher to make a bed.

CAMPFIRES AND COOKING

A camp without a campfire is like a home without a heart. It's the place where everyone gathers not only to eat and keep warm, but also to create that magical sense of 'togetherness' that makes camping so unique. If you decide to make a campfire with no artificial aids like matches or firelighters, divide up responsibilities so that some of you are collecting tinder, kindling and fuel for the wood-stack while the others are clearing a site and building the fire. Keep your campfire area well away from trees, undergrowth, tents, sleeping bags and anything else that might catch a stray spark and smoulder away.

TINDER, KINDLING AND FUEL

A good source of tinder is the key to a good fire. Your tinder will need to ignite at the slightest provocation, so wool or strips of camera film can be very useful to keep in a survival kit. Otherwise you will need to gather whatever is available, which must be fine, fibrous and bone dry. Dry grasses and leaves, pine needles or dried fungi – like the King Alfred's Cakes which grow on dead ash trees – all make excellent tinder in the right (dry) condition. If the ground is damp, look for tinder in the nooks and branches of trees where it will be drier, or use scrapings from the inside of silver birch bark, which will take a spark even when wet.

The A-frame concept can also be used to make a raised bed that will keep you clear of the cold ground and away from any bugs and creepy crawlies.

Kindling is the part of the fire that will burn once the tinder has caught and should be of small, dry twigs. You can make fire-sticks by whittling back the bark of small sticks so there is more surface area to take the flame.

The main fuel should be of larger pieces of wood. Hardwoods like beech, oak, holly, ash and silver birch burn slowly and very hot and are good for cooking food, while softwoods, like conifers, cedar, chestnut and sycamore burn quicker but give out more light. Avoid willow, which is often damp and doesn't burn well.

FIRE TYPES

Some campfires are better for cooking and some for gathering around for a singsong. Cooking fires need a solid surrounding structure that will

Fires don't only keep you warm, dry your clothes and keep animals away – they also give you a vital pick-me-up.

keep your pots and pans steady while the food cooks. If your fire is on grass in a field, remove a few spades of turf, which you must remember to replace when you move on.

A fire for cooking will need to burn down reasonably flat so that a cooking pot can easily be laid on top of the embers. Laying logs at right angles to one another is usually the best method. In wet or cold weather, all fires benefit from a platform of small logs or rocks to keep out the dampness of the ground.

TEPEE FIRE

These are shaped like an Indian tepee with the main fuel source built in a tripod around the tinder kindling inside. The flames will lick up through the central chamber like the draw of a well-ventilated chimney. Tepee fires provide a lot of light, but can burn quickly and their shape is not ideal for cooking.

CRISS-CROSS FIRE

Layers of small logs at right angles to one another throw out a lot of heat and settle well into a deep layer of embers that are perfect for cooking. Place some logs or some stones on either side to support your cooking equipment.

KEYHOLE FIRE

A campfire built of stones in the outline of a keyhole can be adapted to both cooking and sitting around. Build a tepee fire of softwood in the top part of the keyhole and use the lower end as a platform for cooking with a criss-cross fire of hardwood. I like this one – it always looks great, does two jobs and really works well!

TRENCH FIRE

This is an excellent alternative in high winds. Dig a trench about 30 centimetres deep and wide and a metre long, which should be lined with stones. These can then be buried later and will provide

a source of ground heat all night long. Be careful not to use wet, porous rocks, like sandstone, and avoid any rocks near water, as they can explode.

REFLECTORS
Placing a screen, either made of wood or rock, on the side of the fire can act as a windbreak, as well as reflecting heat back towards the fire and the group sitting around it.

TARP SHELTERS

Tarps are incredibly useful items on any trip into the wilderness as they are lightweight and can be used for many purposes, including a makeshift shelter. You can easily construct a rainproof shelter in minutes with a tarp, some cord and a knife. The Aussie army still use a simple tarp construction called a 'hootchie', which was first used during jungle operations in the Second World War.

Tie cord between two trees or push some uprights into the ground. Keeping a section on the ground as under-bed protection, drape the tarp over the cord. Keep it weighted on the ground end with heavy stones and tie cord through both corners of the roof end, pulling

them taut before pegging into the ground. Keep the tarp taut at all times and at a steep angle to the ground so any rain will run off quickly.

CAVES

Caves are entrancing places, but always be careful if you set up camp in one. In an emergency they can be a fantastic place to hole up (literally), but make sure that the cave is not home to other creatures who might not be so keen on having you around. Bears, bats, snakes, rats, crabs and insects aplenty like caves too and may not want to share them with you.

Make sure that your chosen cave isn't prone to flash flooding or, if you are on the coast, open to the rising tide. Test the floor to see how damp it is. Also beware of stale air and don't explore too far inside without proper equipment as you might find yourself trapped by a rockfall. If you have checked out all the possibilities and still feel comfortable, go right ahead and make camp in the cave, but be sure to build your fire outside unless you want to smoke yourself out!

Fishing

An Ancient and Skilful Art

I'D LIKE TO START by saying that I am not a fishing bore! I have endured quite a few evenings in my life being talked at by people who have more fishing jargon and gear than can ever be considered sane. Somehow the more such fish-snobbery I encounter the more turned off I become because I know that at heart, fishing is one of the most pure, ancient and skilful arts on earth and not a competition in one-upmanship over kit.

For me, fish-snobbery (meaning all the gear but little idea) dampens the raw, simple appeal of fishing that I love so much. So you won't get any jargon from me. What I am interested in is the beautiful, sensitive art of fishing itself: learning to beat the fish at their own game; outsmarting them in their own territory; learning to think like they do, and using that knowledge to win.

Half the fun of fishing is the peace and quiet and time-out that it affords. If you rush, you fail. Fishing rewards the smart and the patient. It is not about brute strength, it is about guile. There are no short cuts. I like that.

I remember as a young boy fishing with my late father in Scotland. We used to fish on opposite banks, separated by a few hundred yards. I would settle into the reeds and carefully float a fly over a still, shady pool and wait. I loved the game of cat and mouse, it brought out the hunter in me; and I longed for a fight! I remember looking upstream every now and then, only to see a giant clump of reeds being thrashed mercilessly, with Dad in the middle huffing and puffing in frustration over a hooked fly.

It always made me laugh, and after a while we'd eat our packed lunch together on the bank. These were priceless times. It wasn't the fishing that made it special, but the times spent together enjoying nature. It somehow always felt so right.

I do the same thing now with my sons. They love to come out with me, and Jesse, my five-year-old, staggers along the riverbank under the weight of his fishing bag. We sit on a small bridge and cast and try and work out where the fish might be. Marmaduke, my youngest, wears my father's giant old flip-up sunglasses so that he can see through the glare of the water. He looks ridiculous, but somehow there is great healing in the unbroken continuity of sitting with my sons, the way my father sat with me.

I will never forget the first fish Jesse caught, from a small rowing boat in Scotland, along the same coastline on which I had met my wife Shara

The art of fly fishing requires patience, guile and flair.

Shara and Jesse fishing in Scotland – waiting to catch your first fish requires patience ... try not smiling when it actually happens.

years earlier. We were all in this little boat, casting away, chatting, waiting, rowing and eating. Suddenly his line got a bite. I have never seen anyone look so shocked and excited all at once. He reeled in this small brown trout, and we ate it as pâté that night. Life doesn't get much better.

I have since fished all over the world: with home-made line, home-made rods, nets made from my shirt and from my pants. I have fished with guts as bait, with sand as bait, I have fished with poisonous leaves, I have fished with a home-made bow and arrows. I have caught fish by beating the surface with a stick, I have fished through the ice of frozen lakes, I have dived for fish with spears, fished with knives by flame light with jungle tribesmen and done battle with sting rays, octopus, eels and piranha.

It is all the same game: using our brains to come up with ways to outsmart one of the most sensitive creatures on earth, in their own arena. And I love that challenge.

FISH TALES

Humans have always fished: originally for food, but later for sport. Most of the evidence of ancient fishing techniques has been found on coastlines where nets made of plant fibres, like flax, were used from earliest times. The first primitive hook, known as a 'gorge', was made of a small length of bone, flint or shell sharpened at both ends. This was covered with bait and fed out on a hand line.

The Ancient Egyptians, whose tomb paintings show the first known use of rods and lines, used

The first primitive hook, known as a 'gorge', was made of a small length of bone, flint or shell sharpened at both ends.

Believe me when I say people have been fishing for years!

of songs, poems, folklore, recipes and philosophizing, including details for catching many different species of fish and celebrating the joys of the angler's life.

The original edition was far from being 'compleat', however. Walton published five updated editions in the next 25 years, expanding the original thirteen chapters to twenty-one. The final edition includes a section on fly fishing by his friend Charles Cotton, with the first detailed descriptions of fly-fishing techniques and sixty-five different types of fly.

The book is also famous for its worldly-wise observations on fishing, many of which are still quoted today.

O, sir, doubt not that angling is an art; is it not an art to deceive a trout with an artificial fly?

FLY FISHING

The skill of fishing with rod and line depends as much upon an understanding of fish behaviour as it does on the mastery of a whole range of skills – from setting up the basic tackle to casting, playing the fish and landing it. And, as Walton so vividly described, as much of the pleasure of fly fishing comes from the enjoyment of the solitude of the countryside as it does from the knowledge that you have outwitted the fish in his own environment.

An experienced fly fisherman is able to study the surface of a river and read its contours and subtle signs like a map. He can predict the likely hiding place of his prey depending on the weather, the time of day, and the species of fish he has in his sight.

The art of fly fishing is being able to trick the fish into believing that an artificial fly made of feathers and a hidden hook is actually its favourite dish of the day. This may vary from a mayfly to the pupae of a caddis fly, from a

hooks made of copper. Later, the Chinese used silk to make fishing lines with rice as bait. But while the history of fishing is in many ways the story of the changing methods and materials used to catch fish, those who fish for sport are still faced with the same challenges as those earliest fishermen. Then, as now, an intimate knowledge of the environment and a close study of fish behaviour were the keys to becoming a successful fisherman.

THE COMPLEAT ANGLER

One of the most popular books of all time, *The Compleat Angler* by Izaak Walton, was published in 1653 and has been reprinted more than 600 times in its 350-year history. This meandering tale tells the story of a fowler, a hunter and a fisherman reminiscing and trading knowledge as they travel through the countryside.

The book is a pot-pourri of the ways of the English countryside in a bygone era and is full

The spirit of fishing is a oneness with the living world around you.

Making your own flies is an exacting task, but will enable you to produce the most effective lures for your home fishing patch.

dragonfly to a freshwater shrimp. But it is not as simple as it sounds, as you will be up against some of the wiliest and most sensitive creatures in nature.

There are two main categories of artificial flies: dry flies and wet flies. Wet flies are designed to attract fish below the surface of the water while dry flies are designed to float on the surface. Dry flies are generally used in the summer when the fish are attracted to the surface to feed on insects.

These two types are also divided up into 'Attractors' and 'Deceivers'. The former are designed to provoke an aggressive response in a predatory species like a pike and are often large and garish in colour, while the latter are usually smaller and more subtle in colour and look more like the fishes' natural food.

Flies are generally made of the feathers of common birds like pheasant, duck, hens and turkeys and are carefully constructed to mimic the various parts of the fish prey, namely head, wings, body and tail. While many fishermen buy ready-made flies, the art of making them yourself is well worth mastering. It requires a bit of practice, but it can pay big dividends for the angler who knows his favourite river well and is prepared to put the time in to create a fly that is perfectly suited to his home patch.

Many species of freshwater fish can be caught on a fly, but the most popular by far are two old favourites that can be found in rivers all over northern Europe and the US.

While many fishermen buy ready-made flies, the art of making them yourself is well worth mastering.

Flies, designed to look like natural fishfood.

New Zealand over the last 150 years. Its colour can vary widely depending on environmental factors but is usually dark brown on its back fading to yellowy orange on its belly. Brown trout can vary in size from under a pound up to as much as 25 pounds.

SALMON

The life cycle of the salmon, hatching in fresh water and then migrating to the sea before returning to its birth river to spawn, makes it a unique prize. The most sought after variety for fly fishermen is the Atlantic salmon, not only for its tasty flesh, but for the fact that when it returns to freshwater rivers to spawn it does not feed, which makes it extremely difficult to seduce into a bite.

Wherein lies the true secret and skill of the dedicated fly fisherman.

Brown trout: fly fishing favourite.

Salmon: the ultimate prize.

TROUT

The most widespread species of wild trout is the brown trout which can be found all over temperate latitudes in the northern hemisphere, but also in southern latitudes where it has been introduced in locations from South America to

WILD FISHING

Fishing in the wild using just materials you can scavenge and your wits to help you is one of the most challenging – and satisfying – of all outdoor activities. Lines can be fashioned from twisted bark, plant fibre like nettle stalks, or strands of

clothing or cord (the inside strand of a paracord is one I use a lot), while hooks can be made out of wood, bone, pins or thorn bushes. Wild fishing may mean trapping, spearing or even tickling a fish into allowing you to catch it with your bare hands.

Without modern technology to help, you will have to tune into nature's clues to guide you to the best place to drop your hook or build your fish trap. Understanding fish behaviour will be half the battle. Remember that fish like to feed just before dawn and just after sunset, while all wily fishermen know that a full moon is also a fruitful time.

In summer, they seek out cool, often deeper, water while in the autumn they will be looking for somewhere warmer and perhaps shallower. In fast flowing rivers, fish may seek out areas where the current is not so strong or where a river flows into a lake and the water has more oxygen. Look for minnows jumping, as they may be being chased by larger fish, or swarms of insects over the surface of the water that might attract feeding fish in the water below. Bigger fish also seek out hiding places like the shadows of boulders or under tree trunks where they can prey on smaller fish, and shortly after it has stopped raining is always a good time to get fishing.

FISH TRAPS

Fish traps are one of the most effective ways of catching fish in the wilderness. In fact, nature has her very own version, which anyone who has wandered along the seashore at low tide looking for the stranded residents of rock pools will know.

Fish traps are essentially a technique for persuading fish to swim into an area from which they cannot escape, so you can harvest them at will and keep them fresh for the campfire. Time spent observing the direction in which the fish are swimming and where they congregate will always pay dividends later. In freshwater rivers or lakes, this can be done by building barriers of rocks, so that the fish are forced to swim up a channel into shallower water.

In deeper water, it may be necessary to construct a mesh of saplings that can be pushed into the riverbed. This needs to be dense enough to let the water through but not the fish, and is usually more effective when constructed in sections before you put it in the water.

I caught several trout a few weeks ago in the Yukon, in northern Canada, by building a small rock dam in a natural inlet on the lake shore. The rock dam was in a funnel shape leading into the inlet with a small gap to allow the fish in. The fish find it easy to get 'funnelled' into the inlet but find it harder to escape. I then waited half an hour, noted the fish inside the inlet then stepped across and plugged the gap with a bundle of willow saplings clumped together. It worked well and I could club the fish in the shallows and eat them fresh from the lake. Perfect!

SPEAR FISHING

Fishing with spears is one of the most ancient forms of fishing and is a technique still practised by many tribal peoples today. By spear fishing I don't mean using a powerful underwater spear gun (that's cheating!), but fashioning one yourself from a sharpened stick.

You will need to find the branch of a tree (a hardwood is best) about two metres long and that is as straight and true as you can find. The point needs to be really sharp. If you can't sharpen the wood you will need to lash some sort of sharpened spike, perhaps made of bone, to the end. If bamboo is available, it can be whittled to a sharp point that should be up to the task.

To be a successful spear fisherman, you will require the instincts of a hunter. Your movements in the water must be slow and fluid so as not to

disturb the surface and you must be careful not to cast a shadow as the fish will immediately know you are there. Remember too that water refracts light so the fish you are aiming at will be closer to you than it seems. Practise beforehand by throwing your spear at a rock from a range of distances to see how much of an adjustment you need to make.

I harpooned a stingray a few months ago off a desert island reef with a spear I had made. It worked sweetly! (Sadly, the fish tasted pretty bad.)

TICKLING

There is a mystique around fish tickling, partly due to the fact that it's technically illegal in the UK and partly because many people believe it's not actually possible. But it can and does work, although patience is an essential ingredient. And, as with all things in life, when necessity comes calling, people often find they are able to master skills they had otherwise thought impossible. It is easy to choose the wrong moment, the wrong place and the wrong type of fish to tickle. Brown trout are best as they are often found under the overhangs of riverbanks where it is easiest to manoeuvre yourself into position without frightening them away or casting a shadow.

You may have to wait some time for a fish to appear, but when it does, place your hand slowly in the water keeping the movement as slow and fluid as possible. It is critical to approach the fish from behind (i.e. downstream from it), cup your fingers and slowly bring your hand up under its tail. Remember that as far as the fish is concerned your fingers will feel like the gentle 'tickle' of the water flowing under its body. If you are lucky and the fish goes into a trance, you should be able to slowly raise it in the water until you are able to grab it firmly and flip it out onto dry land.

But don't expect miracles too quickly. And remember, fish are most docile when they have swum up into shallow pools where there is not much oxygen so their reactions will be slow and they are easiest to catch. This is the only way I have ever imagined it! Or alternatively you can wade out into the middle of a stream, kick up a lot of silt and muck. The silt will drive the fish to the banks to seek fresh oxygenated water. Downstream of where you have disturbed the riverbed is often a good place to tickle trout. It needs patience, technique and a bit of luck, but you will dine out on the story forever when you succeed!

ICE FISHING

Fishing through ice is one of the most satisfying and simple ways to fish. In northern Scandinavian countries and the Great Lakes area of the US and Canada, it is a popular pastime in winter and the fish in frozen lakes are usually hungry and inquisitive. I have even tried this in Siberia, in minus 35 degrees: the locals are mad for it!

First make a hole in the ice about 30 centimetres wide. The best tool for this is a metal hand drill, although melting the ice with a fire and heated rocks is a possibility in a survival

It's hard to look cheerful after hours spent at minus 35!

situation. (In Siberia all I had was the frozen leg of a dead yak – but that's another story!) Wherever you are, always be extra careful that the surrounding ice is thick enough to take your weight as the hole itself will weaken the structure. Make sure the ice is at the very least 15 centimetres thick and even thicker if the water beneath is fast moving.

Rods used for ice fishing are much shorter than conventional rods, but if you don't have one you will need to make your own rig. Lash two pieces of wood together at right angles with one resting on the ice across the hole and the other – the 'rod' with the line and hooks – attached at right angles in the water. The more hooks you can attach at different depths, the greater your chances of catching something.

If something takes your bait, the 'rod' will pull down one end, sending the other end upright indicating that you have a catch. Remember to stuff the hole with some young saplings or fir to stop it freezing over again.

FLOAT TUBING

Fishing from float tubes is very popular in the US, where it was invented, and it is becoming increasingly popular with fishermen on the Scottish lochs where they can have a great advantage over a boat in terms of manoeuvrability and quietness in a confined area like a reed bed, for example.

A fishing float tube is basically a swanky version of an inner tube from the tyre of a large vehicle like a tractor. The fisherman sits in the inflated inner tube like an armchair and propels himself backwards using flippers while fishing with a short rod. The advantage of float tubing is that it is very unobtrusive and quiet and allows you to reach parts of a lake that might be inaccessible in a boat. It is not to be recommended at sea, however, or in crocodile territory!

Caving

Exploring the Arteries of the Earth

12

THE ENTRANCE TO a cave is the way in to an entirely new world. It is a world of hidden surprises: at one moment claustrophobic then vast, empty then full, uninhabited but then suddenly full of bats. Caves are forged by the power of nature yet seem to whisper quietly, they are cold but make you sweat, forbidding yet compelling. And the truth is that man has hardly even begun to explore what lies under the earth, and has discovered only a fraction of the underground world.

For some, the sensation of being compressed into a tight space by the weight of millennia of rock above you is both thrilling and mind focusing, but for others it can be alarming and disabling. But knowledge dispels fear, and if you can learn about caves and their dangers, as well as what precautions you need to take, they will give you the adventures of a lifetime.

I have been in some truly awesome and very humbling caves on my travels, from vast chasms carved out by underground rivulets in Central American jungles, to giant ice caves deep underneath Patagonian glaciers. For me, being deep underground is intense and there is little else that is as breath-stopping and exhilarating as probing deep underground into the darkness, feeling rock walls untouched by human hands. At times it is as if you are walking inside the very arteries of the earth, as an uninvited, temporary, but privileged visitor.

A few months ago I was deep underground in an old disused gold mine on the Alaskan border. The roof had caved in at places, leaving only tiny air gaps through which I could squeeze, while holding a flaming torch made of burning hessian. I lowered myself down deep shafts on improvised rope until eventually in the pitch black I was walking crouched along tunnels of sheet ice where the water vapour in the air had frozen in the underground cold. All is silent, all is very precarious; and it is intoxicating!

Caves can be extraordinary but they can also be scary and dangerous. The first and most important rule is make sure you know what you are doing, and the second is never go in alone. Make sure you are with someone who is trained in caves, or get trained yourself. Things can and do go wrong and the end result would be a slow and very undramatic death (i.e. the worst sort!). Surely one of man's worst nightmares is to find themselves deep in a cave, torch batteries dead and unable to find their way out. Add to this a factor like the tide coming in, and you can see what I mean when I say caves are unforgiving. But inherent in all this – if you get it right – is the making of some great adventures.

Caves require that you make good decisions at every turn, but therein lies the thrill. Get it wrong in a cave and you will have a battle on your hands. I remember exploring one particular lava tunnel system in Iceland. Above ground the vast flat plains of volcanic rock, often completely covered with moss, hid many of these tubes. Every now and then you would come across treacherous 'skylights', where the tunnel roof had partially collapsed, and thin moss now hid fatal drops into the old lava tubes. Below ground the tunnels had been created by lava flowing down to the coast. Once the lava had passed, all that remained were the giant 'pipes' that the lava had once flowed through.

As I followed one tube deeper and deeper, using a flaming torch made out of some twigs wrapped in sheep fat (that I had scavenged from a carcass!) to see my way over razor-sharp

Caves require that you make good decisions at every turn, but therein lies the thrill.

Caving need not be this intense, especially if you are nervous of tight spaces!

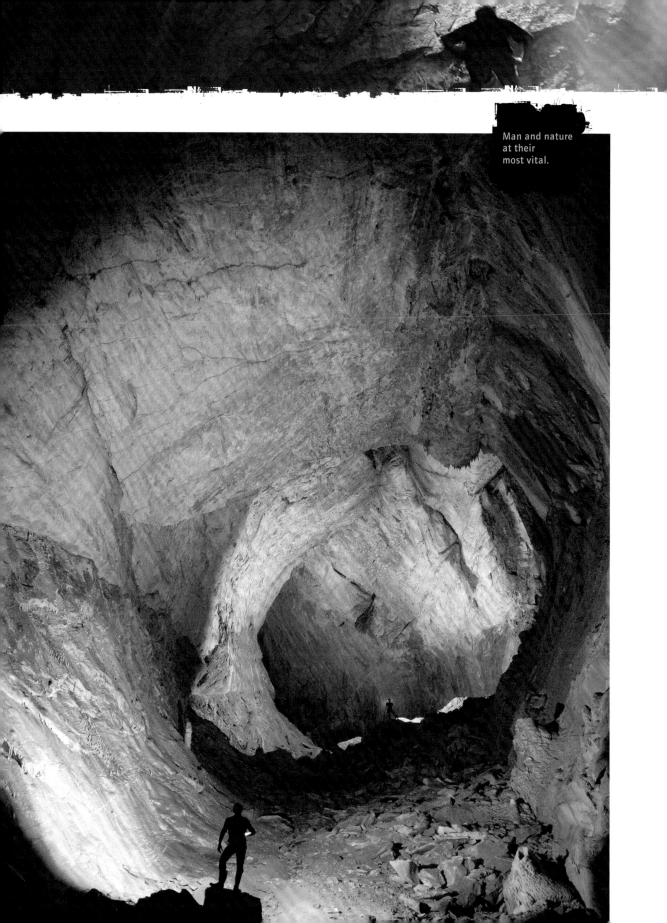

Man and nature
at their
most vital.

volcanic rocks, I came to a place where the tunnel had partially collapsed. There was just enough room to squeeze through before it split into different directions. I marked the floor and wall to show my direction then carried on. But the deeper I went, the less oxygen there was and my hastily made torch was struggling. I started to retreat, but before I could get past the roof collapse, my torch went out. I could no longer see the wall or floor markings showing me my exit.

The world seemed to stand still. The cave was cold, my heart was pounding, the weight of millions of tonnes of rock was directly above me and I was in pitch darkness. This is what I mean when I say caves can focus the mind!

It took ages to weave my way out, and we had to depend on the camera crew's one head torch to guide us to safety. But that had always been the back-up plan, and because we had a back-up plan the adventure was survived and the occasion memorable. That is the key. Have good safety and a well-thought-out game plan, then go for it. Caves require you to allow your body and senses to adjust to the unfamiliar surroundings and when you are scared, stop, think through the sensations and explain them to yourself; take a few minutes to adjust to those feelings then keep moving and keep calm. This is often how I overcome fear. Half of the enjoyment for me is disciplining myself to think calmly when my heart is racing; and for me caves, bats and the darkness inevitably make my heart race! I admit to this readily, but the fear is there to be channelled and to sharpen us for adventure. After all, life is meant to be an adventure or really it is nothing at all. And that adventure doesn't come much bigger and meaner than travelling deep inside a cave.

So, read this chapter carefully, apply the rules and a whole world of subterranean adventure will open up for you.

Under a glacier, looking calmer than I felt.

UNDERGROUND WORLDS

There are many strange worlds to be discovered on our weird and wonderful planet, but perhaps none quite so extraordinary as the world under our feet. Not for nothing have strange beings from dwarfs and dragons to the devil himself been thought to inhabit these complex netherworlds.

But far from being the entrance to the underworld, caves are actually another of nature's spectacular artworks. While they can be formed out of ice inside glaciers or out of lava around volcanoes, the largest and deepest systems have been cut into rock. This rock can be sandstone or even granite, but usually it will be rock that has a high calcium carbonate content, which is soluble in water.

The rock with the highest content of calcium carbonate is limestone, often known as 'karst'.

Karst was formed on the seabed over millions of years in what is known as the Carboniferous Period when the skeletal remains of tiny sea creatures dropped to the bottom of the world's oceans to collect in sediment which over the aeons gradually compressed into the rock we know today as limestone.

Then, with her raw materials in place, the artist got to work. The artist was nature herself. And the tool with which she created these vast underworlds? Water. Water and the simple chemical reactions of a school chemistry set. When rain falls it mixes with the carbon dioxide in the atmosphere to form a solution that is acidic enough to dissolve the calcium carbonate in the limestone.

As sea levels rose and fell over the millennia and the earth's tectonic plates began their mazy dance over the surface of the planet, vast areas of the seabed were lifted above the water to become land. Over millions of years, rainwater started to penetrate the cracks that had formed in the limestone, slowly chiselling away until tunnels and passageways began to form. Later, huge underground chambers as big and grand as cathedrals began to appear, decorated by

Caves are often home to exquisitely shaped rock objects.

most soul-stirring sights are within relatively easy reach of the surface. And with the right training, equipment and safety measures in place, they are ready and waiting for you to take up the challenge.

THE FIRST EXPLORERS

Caves have been inhabited since prehistoric times, offering protection from both the elements and wild animals. One of the treasures that the first cavers found when they began to explore underground in earnest were the cave paintings left by our ancestors from thousands of years ago. Far from being merely ancient graffiti, these paintings, which depict the day-to-day life of our ancestors as they hunted wild animals like the now extinct woolly mammoth, are considered the first works of art.

The earliest known cave paintings are thought to be as much as 32,000 years old, but the most remarkable examples were discovered by four teenagers and their dog, Robot, in 1940 in the Lascaux cave system in southern France. The caves contain more than 2,000 images (although some are now very faint and damaged), dating back 16,000 years and showing wild horses, bulls, bison, stags, wild cats, a bear and a rhinoceros.

glistening chandeliers where the dissolved rock had solidified into strange forms.

And these are what that tight-knit band of subterranean adventurers known as cavers find so compelling. Over the last hundred years, since the first adventurers started exploring the enigmatic tunnels that led away deep underground, thousands of miles of cave systems have been discovered all over the world. Today, virgin cave systems make up some of the last unexplored regions on earth.

Only a minute proportion of these underground worlds will probably ever be seen, but many of the

Lascaux. Cave paintings are the world's first works of art.

and the famous Mammoth Cave in Kentucky (see below) where he succeeded in making accurate measurements of the cave's many different chambers. His travels also took him to the UK where he explored Marble Arch Caves in Ireland and made the first full descent of Gaping Ghyll (see below) in 1895.

Dropping into an 'artery' of the earth: awesome.

SPELUNKING

This is a word that you may well hear bandied about by hardened cavers. And if they're referring to you, it's probably not a compliment. The word comes from 'spelunk', the Old English word for a cave. It was revived in the US in the 1940s to describe young adventurers who enjoyed exploring caves for a hobby. But since then it has come to mean amateurs who start blundering around in caves without any knowledge or training and end up having to be rescued. So, avoid being a spelunker!

EDOUARD MARTEL

Modern caving began in earnest with the Frenchman Edouard-Alfred Martel (1859–1938), who is now known as the 'father of modern speleology'. Speleology is the study of caves for scientific purposes, but the word is sometimes used to mean caving or potholing for fun and adventure. In fact, the two pursuits almost always overlap, as speleologists can hardly help themselves being thrilled by the cave exploration they are undertaking.

Martel is famous for his exploration of caves in France, including the underground river of the Abîme de Bramabiau and the Gouffre de Padirac,

THE CAVING EXPERIENCE

Nothing quite prepares you for those first adrenalin-filled steps into the underground world. The first-time caver will often experience a conflicting whirlpool of sensations including curiosity, exhilaration, wonder and claustrophobia. Shortly followed by sore knees and backache. Sometimes, in the matter of a few minutes, the experience can change from the slimy, dripping world of Gollum in Tolkien's *Lord of the Rings*, into the grand underground palaces of the dwarf lords and their magnificent 'halls of stone'.

Your senses will turn topsy-turvy. Sounds are magnified and their source hard to locate. Water drips first slowly then quickly, now rushing then roaring, sometimes under your feet, sometimes over your head and sometimes echoing eerily from some hidden torrent deep in the rock that surrounds you.

Shadows and strange light effects from your electric torch will disorientate you and often it is impossible to judge distance or the size of a chamber you have just entered. The air feels hot, now cold, now blowing one way and then the other. But when at last you emerge blinking once more into the sunlight, the world under your feet will never be the same again.

The space around you will vary from tiny passageways, 'chimneys', 'bends', 'sumps', and 'boulder chokes' to vast magical chambers decorated with 'speleotherms'. These incredible rock formations look like frozen waterfalls, chandeliers, wedding cakes or glittering candles and are made from dissolved limestone solidifying again into huge stalactites and stalagmites, helictites (a kind of subterranean coral), flowstone, gour pools and cave pearls.

Stalagmites forged over thousands of years deep underground.

Although cavers spend many hours face down crawling through narrow gaps often filled with water and mud or worse, the reward can be the discovery of vast underground chambers decorated with geological forms of extraordinary beauty created by natural processes over hundreds of thousands of years.

PLANNING

If you are smart, your first experience of caving will be in the company of a qualified instructor, usually with a group of other novice cavers. But as you grow more experienced, join a caving club and meet other cavers, you may want to mount expeditions of your own.

Nothing is more important when you venture underground than the process of planning. Gathering as much information as you can beforehand about the area you plan to explore is perhaps more important for caving than for any other type of adventure.

A local guide is invaluable as is a close scrutiny of the weather reports in the days leading up to your expedition. More people become trapped or killed underground by sudden flash floods than any other mishap. You may not know that a storm is lashing the moors above you and water levels underground can become lethal in a matter of minutes.

EQUIPMENT

It is essential to have kit that will keep you warm and dry with your head, feet and knees well protected, and a bombproof light source and back-up. This usually means padded overalls over some thermals, perhaps even a wetsuit; wellington-type boots with a good grip, and a helmet with a torch attached which must be robust enough to withstand knocks and immersions in water and mud.

Later, when you are ready for more advanced caving on underground cliffs or 'pitches', you will need to carry much of the paraphernalia familiar to rock climbers, including harness, ropes, slings, anchors, rope ladders and carabiners.

TECHNIQUES

Smooth and balanced movement when the body is required to stoop, crawl, squeeze and wriggle its way through confined spaces for hours at a time is the secret to effective caving. Many novice cavers find themselves battered and bruised, with the inside of their head under their helmet ringing like a gong, by the time they emerge into the sunlight. The reason is often not the difficulty of the cave itself but their own movement. Slow, fluid, thoughtful movement will always be more effective than a 'bull-in-a-china-shop' approach.

Later in your caving career, when you want to take on more advanced underground features from steep slopes to gaping chasms, you will need to learn many of the techniques of the rock climber, including how to work with ropes, belaying, traversing, abseiling, etc. In the meantime, there will still be much more to discover and enjoy in this brave, new world than you could ever have imagined from the surface.

The advanced caver should be kitted out like a rock climber.

. . . and always be prepared to get wet!

TYPES OF CAVE SYSTEMS

Many of the most awe-inspiring caves on the planet are those made of ice and lava.

GLACIER CAVES

Glacier caves are created by water melting the ice under the surface of the glacier during the summer months to form tunnels, which will freeze again at the onset of winter. These magical ice caverns, with their frozen passageways and columns of sparkling ice, have amazing otherworldly features that make you feel like you've stumbled into the lair of the White Witch in the *Narnia* novels. An ice cave that has formed in the same place two years running will be completely transformed during the second year. The floor under your feet looks like a crystal-clear river frozen in motion while water vapour forms magical frost crystals, frost feathers and ice plates on the walls and ceiling.

I remember one glacial cave in Canada that I was in recently where the floor was a crackling mass of tiny ice cubes. When I trod carefully on one part of it, the floor cracked to reveal a bottomless tube beneath my feet, down which

Glacial caves – one of the most dangerous sort as they are constantly moving, shifting and collapsing.

Once the flowing lava has gone, underground lava tubes often still remain.

the ice cubes funnelled away quickly into blackness. Go down one of these ice tubes and you will never emerge. We witnessed a man killed like this in the Himalayas once and it must be a terrible, terrible way to go.

LAVA TUBES

Lava tubes, by definition, only exist in volcanic regions. They are formed by boiling lava continuing to flow after the layer above has cooled into a solid crust. These underground lava rivers later empty as the flow of molten lava from the volcano begins to dry up. In its place are left extensive tunnels that have many of the same features of limestone caves including stalactites, stalagmites, helictites and flowstone. The longest lava tubes in the world (more than 48 kilometres long) are found on the island of Hawaii. I have been deep inside these tunnels and they are amazing (and scary!).

MECCAS OF THE UNDERWORLD

Many people have no concept of the size and beauty of the worlds that exist under our feet. While some are open to the public, these are usually close to the surface to allow easy access and the use of the artificial lighting required to light them. But – like the world's highest mountains – others are the domain only of those who are willing and able to put up with the discomforts and physical skill required to access them.

SARAWAK CHAMBER, BORNEO

This is the largest natural underground chamber in the world, and was discovered by three Britons in 1981 in Gunung Mulu National Park, Sarawak, on the island of Borneo. Known as 'Good Luck Cave', it is more than 600 metres long, 400 metres wide, 100 metres high and takes more than an hour to cross. It has also been calculated that the chamber could hold ten jumbo jets.

The park is also home to Deer Cave, the world's largest cave passage with a 60-metre high water curtain pouring continuously from the roof. It also features the world's largest cave river passage, Clearwater Cave, along with some spectacular dripstone and flowstone formations in many others.

GAPING GHYLL, YORKSHIRE DALES, ENGLAND

Britain's most famous cave is a 105-metre vertical pothole on Ingleborough Mountain in the Yorkshire Dales. Into this plunge the waters of

A welcome burst of warmth and illumination from the sun.

Fell Beck, creating the highest waterfall in the country. The floor of the chamber was first reached by Edouard Martel in 1895 (see above) using wood and rope ladders.

Twice a year, usually over the May and August Bank Holidays, members of two local caving clubs lower fee-paying members of the public into the main chamber, which is specially floodlit for the occasion. Gaping Ghyll was thought to be the deepest cave chamber in Britain until the recent discovery of the 141-metre high Titan shaft, which connects to old mine workings near Castleton in Derbyshire.

MAMMOTH CAVE, KENTUCKY, USA

Mammoth Cave in Kentucky is the longest known cave system in the world with nearly 600 kilometres of passageway. The caves were discovered around 4000 years ago by local Indians who used cane torches to search for the minerals they used as medicines. A number of mummified bodies have been discovered at the site including one of a man who was killed when a boulder he dislodged fell on him.

A 20-mile section of the cave is open to the public. Features on display include vertical shafts and massive chambers, a 23-metre calcite curtain called Frozen Niagara, gypsum 'flowers' and crystals frozen into transparent needles.

CALL OF THE ABYSS – KRUBERA-VORONJA CAVE

The world's deepest known cave, the Krubera-Voronja Cave, is located in Georgia in the Arabika Massif of the Gagra Range, near the east coast of the Black Sea. Translating as the 'Crows' Cave' in English, the system is the first in the world to be explored to a depth of more than 2 kilometres. And that is probably only the beginning!

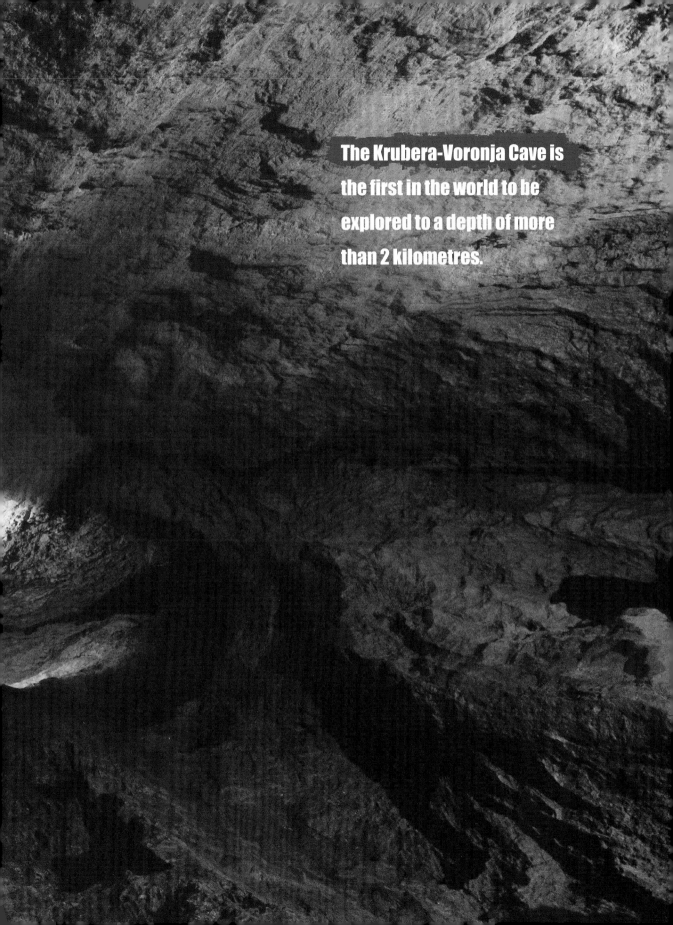

The Krubera-Voronja Cave is the first in the world to be explored to a depth of more than 2 kilometres.

Swimming and Surfing

Immersing Yourself in the Elements

13

urself in

IF TRUTH BE TOLD, it is essential to be able to swim if you are going to experience many of the great adventures there are to be had on our planet. Not only because many of them involve lakes, lagoons, seas, rivers or rapids, but also because adventures so often end up with either a river crossing or an accidental dunking at some point! If you are an adventurer, not being able to swim reduces your options considerably. So, if you can't swim, learn! And, if you find swimming scary, persevere and endeavour to overcome your fears and master the skills required.

Once you can swim, it is essential to understand the dangers of water. People generally drown out of ignorance; and almost always it is ignorance as to the power of water, in terms of currents – 'strainers' in rivers, and rip tides at sea.

I remember once trying to cross a river in the Indonesian jungle. It was in full spate and the water was a menacing dark brown colour. A raging torrent was pounding down the ravines. I was aware that the big danger of jungle rivers is what is unseen: the trees and branches that are jammed or wedged in between rocks under the surface. These obstacles, hidden under the water, act as lethal entrapments. I knew it was going to be risky but once I got into the water it was even

Water is powerful enough to throw you around like a rag doll, pin you where it chooses and let you up only when it cares to.

more powerful than I had envisaged. I was hurtling downstream, clinging to a log with a raft behind me from where the TV crew were filming. Suddenly, a big 'hole' swallowed me up, and then spat me out. I bounced over a hidden trunk, smashing my knee in the process as another load of white water dumped right down on top of me. Just as I was coming up for a breath, the raft then swung on top of me and I disappeared again under water. I was now battered, disoriented and low on puff – big time! Luckily I caught a line hanging off the raft and managed to pull myself free, but I was definitely at the point where things could have swung quite quickly the wrong way!

Water is powerful enough to throw you around like a rag doll, pin you where it chooses and let you up only when it cares to. Never mess with big river rapids, unless you know what you are doing or have the right safety in place. They can kill in the blink of an eye.

The sea is the same. I remember once being dropped from a helicopter beyond the big pounding surf off the Namibian Skeleton Coast. Sailors call this coast the 'Gates of Hell' as they know that even if you make it through the breakers and rip currents, the parched heat of the desert will kill you in hours. I was perhaps only 500 metres offshore but the currents were intense. It took me ages and ages

of careful, controlled swimming, always diagonal to the shore, even to get through the rip and into the breakers. And that was where the adventure really began. The breakers were massive. They weren't the sort of waves that roll you in gently. They were 'dumpers', that simply picked you up then dropped you down into a razor-sharp reef below. I eventually emerged, having swallowed half the south Atlantic, with pockets bulging with sand and rocks that had collected there as I was cartwheeled ashore.

Make no mistake – messing about in big breakers or river rapids is a dangerous sport. Like many fun things, part of the enjoyment is that element of risk. But the key is to understand that risk, maintain a super healthy respect for the power of the water and have a back-up plan in case you need help. Then, get out there and enjoy!

It's the same with surfing. If you can find a great reef break, with reliable, safe sets of waves coming ashore, then learning to 'ride' them is as natural as it comes. Whether you are on a surfboard or a body board, the principle is the same. You are harnessing a great natural phenomenon – the lunar pull on the ocean that creates the tides and waves – and then riding them home. I always get a bit nervous surfing for one reason; I suspect if I spent more time

... even the birds are at it!

doing it, then I would get truly hooked, and everything else would suffer! But hey, that's a pretty good endorsement in itself for the fun there is to be had surfing waves.

I am going to finish this intro by saying that swimming is also a great way to get fit. One particularly gruelling exercise we did in the Special Forces was to be dropped off from a fast insertion speedboat at night, in full kit, at high speed, with a long swim ashore. But it helped get us strong, made our bodies flexible and built good endurance. (And in winter it was a sure way of getting pneumonia! But that's another story.)

We now own a small island off the Welsh coast and I often try and swim around the whole island at slack tide. It takes a good two hours of hard graft and at the end of it, you really know about it (and continue to do so for the next few days!), but I always emerge feeling invigorated, high and bristling with life – and it's all natural!

So swimming: fun, good for you, and as natural as you can get. But more importantly, it opens the door to a whole host of other aquatic adventures. Enjoy.

WILD SWIMMING

Feeling connected to nature is a core part of all outdoor experiences. And when you're immersed in another element, that connection does not get much stronger. All of life depends on water. Two-thirds of the planet's surface is made up of it along with two-thirds of our own bodies. Not to mention those nine months in the watery cradle of the womb. Swimming is even more natural than walking, and the urge to bathe in water is a unique pleasure that engages the soul completely. And while swimming lengths in the local swimming pool may be a healthy pastime, nothing quite compares with the thrill of finding a cool stretch of river and diving in on a lazy summer's afternoon or under the stars on a hot summer's night.

Nature's watering holes come in all shapes and sizes. From huge, peaty rivers on high moorland rushing beneath mountain peaks to the mazy meanderings of brooks and streams making their way lazily through woods of oak and ash, past flower meadows and flood plains, before their final outpouring into the sea.

Wild swimming is no less than the art of spontaneity itself. The life force unleashed. A stout heart and a bit of spirit are all that are needed to brave the chilly embrace of a mountain stream with none of the hard-earned skills required to scale a rock face or to keep a paraglider aloft.

And yet that very same impulse to throw caution to the winds and to plunge in without a second thought is the very same impulse that allows us to step out of the well-trammelled habits of everyday life and experience so many of the other great adventures that the outdoors has in store for us.

COLD WATER SWIMMING

Most people associate swimming with the warm waters of summer, but a small but dedicated band of hardy folk believe passionately in both the fun and health-giving qualities of cold water swimming. Swimming in winter seas on Christmas Day or New Year's Day is an annual ritual in many coastal areas of both the UK and the US, attracting large crowds of onlookers muttering to themselves that the participants must be mad. Until later, watching the life-giving effect on those who have partaken, they find themselves regretting they didn't have the guts to dive in themselves.

... yes, and swimming in a place like this is as irresistible as it looks.

Water can spin you, pin you and rarely fails to thrill you.

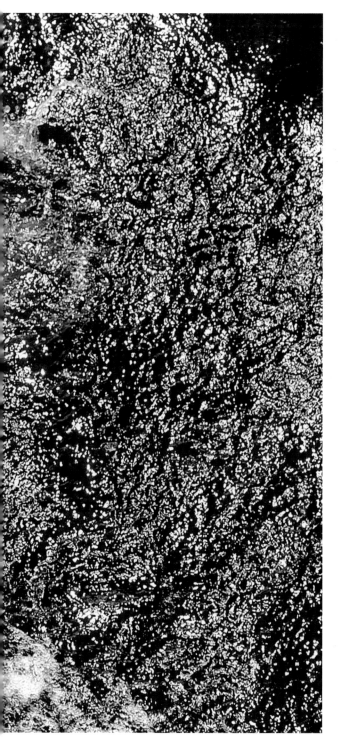

Oh, and it can also freeze you!

I fell in love with Shara while skinny dipping on the north coast of Scotland on New Year's Day. It was freezing cold, half my clothes were being washed away by the waves and Shara helped me gather them. I was hooked (and on the swimming as well!). Since then I have swum on every New Year's Day regardless of where I am in the world. At times that has been quite interesting to say the least!

In Finland, way up in the Arctic Circle, the tradition of cutting a hole in the ice when the lakes and rivers are frozen solid in winter is called *Avantouinti* (literally 'ice-hole swimming'). Together with another Finnish tradition – wood-burning saunas conveniently located next to lakes and rivers – its popularity is currently undergoing a revival with wilderness health spas promising the ultimate cold-water plunge.

Aficionados of cold water swimming claim that not only is it a very effective way of building the body's immune system against illness and reducing blood pressure, but it is also a powerful mental discipline. For a short time at least, the mind can be taught to keep physical discomfort at bay. With the right attitude the cold can be experienced as a form of abstract energy and turned into a positive force that develops stamina, endurance and a healthy mind.

I have had the fortune (or misfortune) to have swum many times in the icy water of frozen lakes.

The crew filming me swimming – and getting in the way!

There's so much fun to be had from canyoning.

The worst was a swim actually under the ice of a frozen lake in Siberia in winter to show how to find your way out if the current takes you under the glassy prison. I was naked and it was minus 30 degrees. But I survived, just; despite my eyeballs freezing and my winkle disappearing!

CANYONING AND COASTEERING

One of nature's more extreme fairground rides – and perhaps the ultimate form of wild swimming – is the sport of canyoning. Known as canyoneering in the US and kloofing in South Africa, canyoning involves following the course of a river through a white water ravine wearing wetsuits and helmets and carrying basic rock climbing equipment for when the going gets tough (or rough!).

The rewards are the simple – the unique joys of rushing water, stunning mountain landscapes and a heady brew of adrenalin-pumping activities including swimming, jumping, scrambling, climbing, slipping, sliding and abseiling.

Most canyoning trips start at the top of a gorge and work their way down in stages. Many of the best sites are in remote areas so it's essential to go with a guide who knows the area well rather than heading off on your own. As with caving and potholing, the main danger is from flash floods, which can funnel down from higher ground with very little warning.

Coasteering is basically the coastal version of canyoning with the added ingredient of a surging sea thrown in for good measure. Its pleasures include the opportunity to explore up close that fine line between the sea and the shore, delving into fissures and caves, swimming under huge cliffs and exploring places into which only seals would normally venture.

SURFING

'Eskimo rolls', 'suckies', 'barrels', 'aerials', 'spin outs', 'point breaks', 'tubes', 'cutbacks', 'thrusters' – there's certainly no shortage of colourful lingo in the world of surfing. And that's hardly surprising because harnessing the power of the waves evokes one of the most powerful feelings of freedom in the outdoors that it is possible to experience and you need new words to describe it. At its purest and most intense, it is just you and Mother Nature out there atop the waves, and for many people surfing is truly an escape into another world.

It's true that the waves can sometimes be crowded, but the thrill of standing up for the first time on a surfboard (and staying up) as the glassy rush of water slips away under your feet lives long in the memory. And, more often than not, it is the beginning of an addiction that gets stronger as the years go on. Many outdoor sports harness the force of gravity to generate movement and speed, but harnessing the power of water and the rhythms of the tides is equally if not even more thrilling.

There is also a life-affirming culture around the sport that attaches itself to you from the moment you tuck a surfboard under your arm and take those first few steps towards the breakers. It has its roots in the carefree antics of the Polynesian islanders of Hawaii whose extraordinary feats on the first surfboards so captivated Captain Cook's men during his epic voyages of discovery, while its modern incarnation found its first flowering in the sun-drenched 1960s revival on the sunshine coasts of Australia and California.

But, believe me, you will never be a real 'surf dude' unless you practise. While the core skills of paddling into the right position, catching a wave, standing up and being able to ride the waves can be mastered quite quickly, it takes months and years rather than days and weeks to get really good.

To be able to study the wind, the weather and the tides and instinctively know how the waves are going to behave and react with the dynamics of the board you are riding is a skill that requires intuition along with great physical skill. And that takes practice. But arriving at your favourite surfing beach two hours before sundown to find a perfect break rolling around the point is one of life's great thrills, and should not be missed for anything.

Boogie boarding – all the thrill with a fraction of the skill.

BOOGIE BOARDING

It fell to Lt James King, the commander of one of Captain Cook's ships, to write the first ever description of what we know today as bodysurfing or boogie boarding:

> . . . *their Arms are us'd to guide the plan[k], thye wait the time of the greatest Swell that sets on Shore, & altogether push forward with their Arms to keep on its top, it sends*

Big wave surfing – one of the boldest, most dangerous undertakings it is possible to do.

them in with a most astonishing Velocity, & the great art is to guide the plan[k] so as always to keep it in a proper direction on the top of the Swel' . . .

The above diversion is only intended as an amusement, not a tryal of skill, & in a gentle swell . . . must I conceive be very pleasant, at least they seem to feel a great pleasure in the motion which this Exercise gives.

It is now thought that surfing, both standing up and in the prone position, on long planks of woods or bundles of reeds and palm fronds was a common practice among the South Sea islanders for centuries before the arrival of the Europeans. And as Lt King clearly thought when he wrote his diary entry in 1779, surfing face

down above the waves can be one of the most exhilarating experiences.

OK, so you might not be able to take on the monsters ridden by the big-wave surfers, but don't forget that boogie boards can provide hours of fun and because you're flat and face down when you catch the wave, it's a far easier skill to master. The key to it all is timing. Launch yourself too early or too late and you will miss the wave. The usual mistake people make is to leave it too late, but you'll know when you've timed it perfectly when that massive surge of acceleration picks you up and throws you towards the beach.

Although the beauty of bodysurfing is that almost everyone is capable of giving it a go, watch out that you don't get carried away. There may well be more experienced 'real' surfers further out who may lull you into a false sense of security. Always remember they will probably be wearing wetsuits and using a buoyant longboard to keep them safe from dangerous currents and undertow. So never underestimate the power of the water, keep reasonably close to the shore and choose medium-sized waves. They will still be quite powerful enough to give you the ride of your life!

NOVICE BOARDS

If you're new to the world of wave riding, the temptation will be to go straight out there and buy the most stylish gear you can find and which all the cool surfers are using. Resist the temptation. Surfing is a skill like any other and choosing the appropriate (not most fancy) equipment when you're a novice will help you improve far quicker than if you're struggling with gear that's too advanced for your skill level. Remember – don't become an 'all the gear, no idea' man!

Balance is one of the keys that will unlock the world of surfing and to gain confidence your first board needs to be very stable and very buoyant.

Length is a vital factor and a novice should look for a board that is between 75–90 centimetres longer than he or she is tall. This will provide the most stability. A lot of boards have three fins these days, but one is quite enough when you're starting out – and it means there'll be fewer sharp points to worry about when you're crashing about in the surf.

FUNBOARDS
Wider, chunkier, and longer than a surfer's shortboard (see below), funboards are perfect for beginners as they are stable and manoeuvrable and especially good in surf which is not too powerful (i.e. the type of waves that are best to ride when you're a novice).

POP-OUTS
These boards get their name because they are generic copies of custom-made designs and 'pop-out' from the machine mould in which they are made. OK, so you won't be competing in the World Championships on one of these but they are far cheaper, much more robust, and a lot more stable than the handcrafted models the experts use. They're perfect for first-timers.

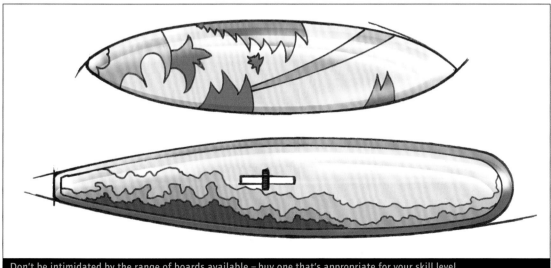

Don't be intimidated by the range of boards available – buy one that's appropriate for your skill level.

SOFT BOARDS

Soft boards are made of polyurethane foam rather than fibreglass. This means they are very stable and buoyant, and they won't knock you out during the inevitable wipe-outs.

'DUDE' BOARDS

LONGBOARDS

These are the original Californian surfboards made famous by the Beach Boys and the sun-bleached hippies that surfed the breaks at Malibu on America's West Coast in the 1960s. Often more than 3 metres in length, longboards have a distinctive rounded front end called the 'nose' and due to their bulk are difficult to manoeuvre. For the more experienced, though, longboards are the ultimate tool for graceful wave riding.

SHORTBOARDS

If you're out to impress on the beach this summer, a custom-made shortboard will be your board of choice. They are built with a bewildering range of design options from the nose to the tail and the fin, not to mention the 'rocker' – the profile of the curve on the underside of the board. Unless you're a fully fledged surfie – and have money to burn – watch out because shortboards are the Ferraris of the waves and require great skill to ride.

THE SEVERN BORE

Whether it's on a longboard, a shortboard, or even a boogie board with a good pair of flippers to propel you along, one of the world's most unusual surf breaks is the bi-annual tidal wave known as the Severn Bore.

Bores are created by high tides funnelling through a deep, wide estuary into a narrow, shallow river. And one of the world's best and most consistent examples is to be found on the Severn River in Gloucestershire in the UK. The reason for the phenomenon is that the Severn has the second

... and the sea looks quite appealing as well!

Don't be dazzled by the colours – choose kit suitable for you.

largest tidal range in the world at nearly 15 metres. So on the highest spring tides of the year – in March and October, ideally in combination with a low-pressure system and a following wind – the full force of the Atlantic funnels into the mouth of the river and travels 20 miles upstream before dissipating at Gloucester Weir.

The result is a perfect wave that has been known to reach 3 metres high, which travels at up to 12mph and which remains unbroken for mile after mile. Unsurprisingly, it is a magnet for surfers, bodyboarders and kayakers. The current unofficial record for a ride on the Severn Bore is a ride of nearly an hour, covering more than 12 kilometres. For reasons not entirely understood, the biggest bores come in nine-year cycles.

There are around sixty bores around the world including the Indus, the Amazon, and the mother of them all, the Qiantang River in China. The roar of the Qiantang in full flight can be heard more than 24 kilometres away and the wave has been known to reach nearly 9 metres high with a speed of 40kph. Perhaps unsurprisingly, it is known locally as the 'Silver Dragon'. Now try that for size!

Surfing the Severn Bore – one of the longest waves you'll ever ride.

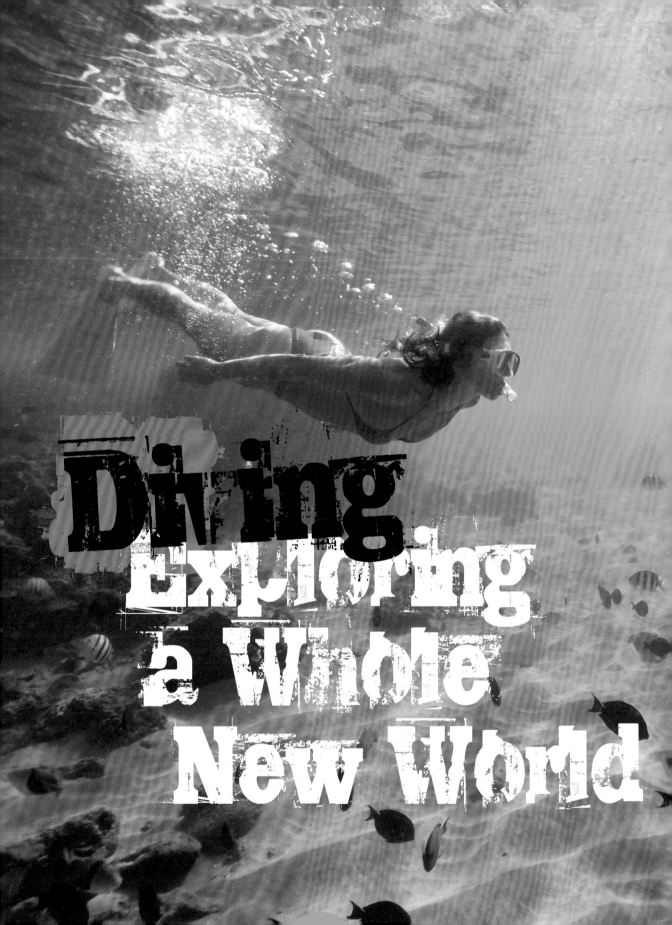

Diving
Exploring a Whole New World

14

IN THIS LIFE we are all blessed with the chance to enjoy three great outdoor spaces for adventure: land, air and water; and all three have the potential for an obscene amount of fun! To miss out on any one of them is quite simply an opportunity missed, but in my view, the underwater world combines the most exhilarating with the most relaxing and peaceful of all.

Considering we are all carried around in a sack of fluid for nine months before we are born, it is hardly surprising that humans gain such pleasure from the sensation of weightlessness and such relaxation from the quiet that water affords. I found it so cool to see how naturally both my young sons loved the water as tiny babies. They would swim (or rather be held in my arms) in the sea or in a pool and be 100 per cent comfortable. When I ducked underwater with them, they would be calm and wouldn't struggle, and as I emerged they would still be looking pretty relaxed. Now that can take some adults a lifetime to master!

Fear of water in adults generally comes from some traumatic experience when they were young, but a big help in overcoming this fear is understanding the rules of the game. First of all remember that knowledge dispels fear, so learn where the real dangers are and where they are not. For example, once you can swim then the depth of the water should not be a concern – there is no practical difference between having 3 metres and 3000 metres of water beneath you. It is all relative. Likewise with dangers; and here the key is always being aware of the potential power of water, whether it is rivers, the surf or out at sea.

Once you dip your head under the surface of the open sea, it really is a whole new world. One of my great joys is freediving with no sub-aqua kit (or even clothes when I can get away with it!). For me that is diving at its most pure. I have learnt that it takes a while to get your lungs 'stretched' to allow you to stay down for a good length of time, but once that ability and that confidence

Diving allows you to enter that mystical and tranquil world beneath the waves.

comes and you can control your heart rate to beat slowly and calmly, it really is pure magic.

I have had the great privilege of freediving in some truly exquisite remote islands around the world. Joining the realm of the fishes, becoming like them, hunting, exploring, almost 'dancing' underwater, is one of my favourite passions. I once dived on a deep reef off an island in the South Pacific and on my first dive I knew the reef was as far down as I could go on one breath. But after half an hour or so my lungs slowly adapted and stretched and I could then comfortably explore the coral tunnels and cliffs. Unencumbered by scuba kit, you can move truly free and weightless, arching and curving as you swim. Such moments are surely close to heaven.

On another occasion though (of over-enthusiasm), when I had been freediving all day, every day for a week, I did end up in hospital coughing up blood, which put a bit of a dampener on things! But don't let that put you off. Bear in mind that in the months preceding my stay in hospital, I had taken my lungs to 8848 metres on Everest and had freedived probably too deep, too often, and all after a series of long-haul flights. (I was also smoking a bit in those days (idiot!), so a stint in hospital was probably on the cards.)

Or, of course, you could go scuba diving. The benefit of using scuba kit is simply that you extend those wonderful underwater moments. You don't need to surface every few minutes to take a breath and you can fully explore the underwater world in relative comfort. And working buddy-buddy with someone like this is in many ways more fun as well as being a

uniquely bonding experience. In fact, I very rarely meet fellow scuba divers whose eyes don't start shining when you ask them about the joys of diving and I challenge you to surface from a dive without a smile on your face – and that's generally a good benchmark to use!

DAVY JONES'S LOCKER

Finding the key to Davy Jones's Locker was no easy task! Since the days our ancestors first began crossing the oceans, man had been given tantalizing glimpses of the strange world beneath the surface. But only for as long as it was possible to hold a single lungful of air. It wasn't until the middle of the twentieth century that the problem of how to breathe underwater for a significant length of time was finally solved.

The challenge was how to get a continuous air supply to a diver at depth. The first idea was recorded in the fourth century BC by the Greek philosopher and writer Aristotle, who described an upside-down bronze tank which retained air when submerged and into which the diver put his head. But those early experiments were limited both in terms of the depth that could be reached and how much a diver could move around.

During the Renaissance, Leonardo da Vinci made drawings of snorkels and air tanks – a significant achievement in itself, but not very practical. There was an important breakthrough in the 1820s when two Englishmen, Charles and John Deane of Whitstable in Kent, designed a diving suit with air pumped into the helmet that was used in salvage work. But at this time, the effects of water pressure on the body were only dimly understood. We know now that water adds pressure by the equivalent of another atmosphere every 10 metres in depth. This means that to counter the added pressure on the lungs, the air breathed in must also be under greater pressure or otherwise the lungs can't be filled.

You can move truly free and weightless, arching and curving as you swim.

There really is a whole new world living submerged.

S.C.U.B.A.

The term 'scuba' is an acronym for the term Self-Contained Underwater Breathing Apparatus. It was the invention of one of these in 1943 in the form of the 'aqualung' by French naval officer Jacques-Yves Cousteau and engineer Emile Gagnan that solved the problem of supplying air to a diver at sufficient pressure regardless of the depth. It also revolutionized a diver's ability to move freely underwater and led directly to the development of the sport we know today as scuba diving.

This remarkable piece of kit allowed divers to breathe air from cylinders mounted on their backs at the same pressure as the surrounding water. Once the problem of how to breathe for lengthy periods of time underwater at depth had been solved, the relatively easy task of controlling buoyancy using a combination of weight belts and life jackets that could be both filled or drained of air as necessary was fairly simple.

More difficult to solve were the potentially lethal effects of breathing pressurized air – which contains both nitrogen and oxygen – on the chemistry of the human body. The deeper the dive, the greater the amounts of nitrogen dissolved into the bloodstream, which, unless released back into the lungs and exhaled, rapidly becomes toxic. Decompression charts were developed so that divers would know from the outset the length of time they could safely stay at any given depth. They would then ascend in stages to allow the nitrogen time to be safely released.

It allowed divers to breathe air from cylinders mounted on their backs at the same pressure as the surrounding water.

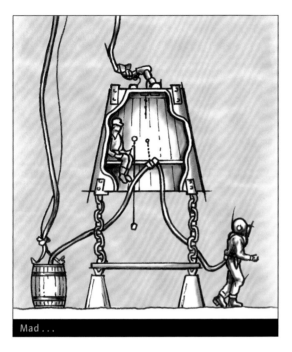

Mad...

...bad...

CAPTAIN COUSTEAU

As well as co-inventing the aqualung, Captain Cousteau pioneered the science of marine

...but the bravest of pioneers.

exploration and became famous for his many documentaries of underwater exploration. A keen amateur film-maker from an early age, he later became Head of the French Navy's Underwater Research Unit during the Second World War. During this period he experimented with underwater photography using a camera in a glass bowl while breathing from a hose connected to the surface. It was his frustration with this inconvenient method of breathing that had inspired him to invent the aqualung.

After the war and with the financial aid of a friend, he salvaged a British minesweeper and converted it into a floating laboratory kitted out with scientific equipment and a film-editing suite. Aboard the *Calypso*, which became one of the most famous boats in the world, over the next fifty years Cousteau circled the globe fifteen times, producing more than forty books and a hundred documentaries, the most famous being the classic TV series *The Silent World*.

Diving in spectacular locations with good friends is the best.

SCUBA DIVING

Learning to dive is a thrilling journey in itself. The only real questions that need answering are where and how to do it. Some people learn while they are on holiday, others prefer to do most of their training in the local swimming pool so there is more time for diving when the long-awaited holiday comes around.

You then have to decide whether you'd prefer a club-based system, learning your skills over weeks or months, or a course completed in a much shorter time either at home or abroad. The advantage of the club system is that you will have ready access to dive buddies, equipment and club dive outings on your home patch when you're qualified.

Two of the largest diving organizations for dive training and certification are the British Sub Aqua Club (BSAC), which operates a club system, and the Professional Association of Diving Instructors (PADI), the largest dive training and certification organization in the world.

Dive training, whether in a club or course environment, will be divided into three main areas: Classroom Theory, Confined Water (pool) training and Open Water experience.

CLASSROOM THEORY

This covers the basic principles of diving, an introduction to the equipment, a basic understanding of the physics involved and the effects of pressure on the human body.

CONFINED WATER

Pool training covers the basic skills required to stay comfortable underwater and be familiar with the equipment – from the basics of masks, fins and snorkels through to wet and drysuits, regulators, cylinders, buoyancy aids and dive computers.

OPEN WATER

Usually conducted in the sea, but sometimes in a lake, this part of dive training allows students to put what they have learnt into practice and gain more experience. Early open water dives are usually in shallow water before progressing to more challenging depths.

THE 'BENDS'

Before the effects of pressure on the human body were fully understood, many pioneering divers died from the 'bends', or nitrogen narcosis, a

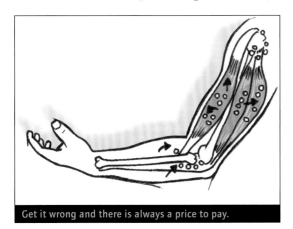

Get it wrong and there is always a price to pay.

condition Jacques Cousteau dubbed the 'rapture of the deep'. The effect of breathing nitrogen under pressure – being 'narced' as it's known – is a bit like being drunk. It affects different people at different depths and in different ways but will usually start having some effect from about 20 metres. At depths below 30 metres, judgement can become severely impaired and divers have even been known to remove their masks in the belief that they can breathe like fish. Generally, this is not a good idea.

Decompression sickness, the 'bends', is caused by surfacing too quickly at the end of a dive before the nitrogen and other gases trapped in the body tissues have had a chance to be released slowly. When they are released too quickly in an uncontrolled ascent, the bubbles 'effervesce' in the bloodstream. Symptoms include severe pain in the muscles and joints, itchy skin rashes, headaches and dizziness. The bends can kill unless a diver is quickly put into a recompression chamber.

REEFS, WALLS, WRECKS AND CAVES

For many the first experience of the underwater world is intoxicating and it's not hard to understand why. The sensation of weightlessness is the nearest most of us will ever get to experiencing the zero gravity of a spacewalk. Some even experience vertigo when diving in clear, tropical waters over an ocean wall! But above all the pristine beauty and enhanced colours of the underwater world will take your breath away.

There are many forms of recreational diving, each with their own attractions and sensations. They range from a gentle shore dive, wading into the sea from the beach, to diving with seals and penguins under the Polar ice.

The most popular diving is found among the coral reefs of the world's tropical regions.

For many, the first experience of the underwater world is intoxicating, and it's not hard to understand why.

Weightless and among the fish → it's true escapism.

Although sometimes mistaken for plants, coral reefs are formed by the skeletal remains of coral polyps that build up on one another to form massive structures that sometimes stretch for hundreds of miles. The most famous example is Australia's Great Barrier Reef. Corals grow into extraordinary shapes, resembling everything from giant brains to deer antlers, and attract all manner of sea life including giant sea fans and sponges and huge schools of multicoloured fish. Reefs often form on the edges of underwater

Although sometimes mistaken for plants, coral reefs are formed by the skeletal remains of coral polyps that build up on one another to form massive structures.

cliffs, known as 'walls', where the seabed can drop away for hundreds of metres. Swimming alongside a coral wall exploring its many nooks, crannies, swim-throughs and overhangs is one of diving's great joys.

Diving on the many thousands of wrecks around the world from Second World War battleships to cruise liners and planes can be like entering a time-capsule. One of the world's most famous wreck sites is Scapa Flow in the Orkney Islands off the north-east coast of Scotland where the German fleet was scuttled in 1919 to avoid falling into Allied hands.

CREATURES OF THE DEEP

Few underwater experiences compare with the thrill of diving with the creatures that inhabit the underwater world. While for some the opportunity to look a Great White shark in the eye at close quarters from behind the steel bars of a cage is the ultimate thrill, for others nothing can beat the joy of swimming gently alongside the rippling wings of a giant manta ray, the caped crusaders of the ocean.

SHARKS

There are many species of shark and not just the ones that might occasionally attack humans. Whatever the type, there is something about a creature that evolution has turned into a ruthless killing machine that haunts the imagination, and diving with sharks of any type is an unforgettable experience. I had the unfortunate experience of accidentally jumping almost directly on top of a 2-metre tiger shark, one of the few man-eaters in the sea, when I was swimming off a home-made raft in the Pacific. I don't intend the experience to be repeated!

. . . but remember who's boss!

The manta ray, the largest of the rays. They are curious around humans and often swim with divers.

WHALESHARKS

The largest fish in the sea, up to 20 metres long and weighing 20 tonnes, whalesharks are also among the gentlest. The main risk for divers is getting in the way of their large and powerful tails. Ningaloo Reef, off Western Australia, is famous for its whaleshark sightings particularly between April and June.

MANTA RAYS

Manta rays are the gentle giants of the ocean, inhabiting coral reefs all over the tropics. The largest known specimens measure up to 7.5 metres across. They propel themselves through the water using a wave motion that ripples along their pectoral fins. Few underwater creatures are more graceful.

FREEDIVING

Diving with scuba equipment opened up a whole new world under the sea. But old habits die hard. For thousands of years, the only way we could glimpse the contents of Davy Jones's Locker was by holding our breath and diving down; and for centuries pearl divers made their living with this very skill, staying underwater for up to five minutes at a time and reaching incredible depths.

Now breath-hold or freediving is regaining its popularity. Unencumbered by bulky scuba gear and without the accompanying rumble of exhaled air bubbles, freedivers can swim among shoals of fish without alarming them. They can also delve into the nooks and crannies of coral reefs without snagging their equipment and damaging the reef. The skill is all about learning to fin differently, to relax and to keep the heart rate

Freediving – the art of exerting control over the impulse to breathe.

The discipline of freediving requires carefully monitored technical training.

down so that oxygen is used more sparingly.

Freediving has also become a serious competitive sport in its own right and there are six official disciplines. These test the competitor's ability to perform a number of breath-hold tasks including holding the breath on the surface, distance swimming in a swimming pool and reaching the greatest depth possible with and without a variety of aids such as weights, belts and fins. The Constant Weight category is considered the purest and the toughest form of freediving. The objective is to swim as deep as possible wearing only fins, mask and a weight belt.

Some of the statistics are indeed truly breathtaking. While records are still being broken with almost every year that goes by, the men's record for breath-holding on the surface is more than 9 minutes (try that next time you're having a bath!) and the deepest depth reached in the 'No Limits' category – where contestants can use weights to descend and an air bag to lift them to the surface – is more than 200 metres.

That's more than twice the height of London's Big Ben!

HERBERT NITSCH

An Austrian world record freediver, Herbert Nitsch (born 1970) has at one time or another held seven out of the eight world records recognized by AIDA, the governing body of freediving, and has dominated the sport since breaking his first world record in 2001.

During his No Limits world record attempt in Spetses, Greece, he reached a staggering 214 metres down. This is the deepest depth ever reached by a diver holding their breath.

Herbert's long-term goal is to freedive to a depth of 305 metres, more than double the depth ever achieved by a scuba diver (150 metres). A professional pilot, Herbert also designs diving equipment and develops innovative new diving techniques in collaboration with medical experts in his home town of Vienna.

TANYA STREETER

Once dubbed the 'World's Most Perfect Athlete', Tanya Streeter (born 1973) has been the holder of many freediving world records, and more recently she has made various TV shows about marine life around the world. Born in the Cayman Islands, she went to school in the UK but discovered her talent for freediving back home in the Caribbean.

Tanya can hold her breath underwater for more than 6 minutes and as a world record holder has reached 122 metres and 160 metres in the Variable Weight and No Limits disciplines respectively. She is now a passionate environmental spokeswoman for the marine environment.

Tanya Streeter: living proof that mermaids exist!

Combining diving and caving is double the excitement but double the danger.

Rafts and Rafting

Awesome Fun on the Water

15

THE FIRST RAFT I ever built was a bit of a disaster; well actually it was quite a big disaster! I was eight years old and a friend of mine and I had built this small raft at home in the Isle of Wight. We launched it in the local harbour at low tide and initially . . . all went well. It floated nicely, but a few minutes later (as if on cue), it started to absorb water and slowly sink beneath us. By this stage we had floated out into the harbour a little way and, predictably, had floated into difficulties! The raft soon sank completely and we both swam for the nearest bit of land. But this bit of land ended up being the soft, clay mud of a low tide harbour – effectively like quicksand. There followed a battle of two kids thrashing around helplessly in sinking mud, getting precisely nowhere. Help eventually arrived in the form of the local coastguards, who delivered a stern, well-deserved reprimand against recklessness. My rafting career was up and running!

Since that early escape, I have been on (and thrown out by big rapids!) home-made rafts all over the world – from the South Pacific to the Rockies, from the Sierras and the Zambezi to the Yukon and the Thames. A few have sunk beneath me, others have been pretty seaworthy . . . but all have been awesome fun! One of my favourites was a raft I built with a friend at school made out of a giant old piece of polystyrene about the size of two sofas. We carved and shaped it into a boat, painted it and set out into the nearby river.

Another fun one was an old bath tub that my best friend Charlie and I rowed recently for over 26 miles down the River Thames through Central London. We were raising money for a friend who had lost his leg in a climbing accident and needed a new prosthetic limb. Charlie and I were naked (well, what do you normally wear in a bath?), and both of us were frantically rowing and trying to balance to stop this thing turning over in the

Not all rafts go according to plan!

One of my favourite pictures, as it sums up all that I hold dear.

tidal waters. We finally arrived at dusk, exhausted and covered in blisters on our hands and bums. But I'm proud to say we got the prosthetic leg for our friend!

That reminds me of another raft I was on in the South Pacific where I ended up being circled by a tiger shark, one of the most aggressive man-eating sharks on earth. Not having spotted the creature, I innocently dived into the sea in order to cool off and landed pretty much straight on top of a 5-metre monster that was cruising just beneath my raft. The shark was as surprised as me, and darted off, giving me a few precious seconds to vault out of the water. It then returned, now seriously cheesed off, and spent ten minutes circling me and thrashing its tail against the raft, before deciding I would make too bony a meal and swimming off.

But the riskiest one has to be the canoe made out of a rotting zebra carcass that I paddled down one of the most densely croc and hippo populated rivers on earth, the mighty Zambezi. I remember floating along in this vast, wide expanse of murky river, watching crocs lining the banks and hippos surfacing every few hundred yards. All I knew was that as far as they were concerned, what I was paddling in was, effectively, lunch.

But don't let my stories put you off, not all rafts need to be as dangerous and ridiculous as these. One of the great pleasures in life is starting out with whatever materials you can find around you, using a bit of sweat and lots of imagination and creating something that will float you down a river, across a lake or out to sea.

Oh, and the best advice I can give is . . . however much buoyancy you think you will need, double it and that'll probably be about right!

THE FIRST RAFTS

Rafts were the first spaceships. When man first felt that primitive and instinctive urge to

explore beyond the limits of the known world, he was confronted with a seemingly insurmountable problem – the sea. Crossing the oceans and discovering what lay beyond was to early man as big a challenge and an adventure as building a spaceship and travelling into space is for us.

And the first primitive craft that ventured out on the early voyages of discovery were all rafts of some kind. A raft differs from a boat in that it floats because the sum of its parts is lighter than water. A boat, on the other hand, uses the displacement principle first formulated by Archimedes, whereby a watertight shell experiences a buoyant lift equal to the weight of the displaced fluid.

A raft can be also be built relatively quickly and easily without tools, by lashing together found materials like wood or bundles of reeds. The first rafts were almost certainly used for transporting people and goods down rivers and over lakes, like those used by the Ancient Egyptians and the famous reed rafts that can still be seen today on Peru's Lake Titicaca. And the first great sea journeys, thousands of years before the great European explorers like Christopher Columbus and Captain Cook, were made on rafts. Stretches of sea in Indonesia, the Mediterranean, in Japan and off California are known to have been crossed as long as 10,000 years ago.

It's sobering to think that all human exploration beyond what could be achieved on two feet began with the invention of the humble raft. No wonder they still have such a magnetic attraction for adventurers the world over.

RAFT DESIGNS

Rafts are the most basic type of sailing craft and use any buoyant materials to keep afloat. Traditional designs used available materials like balsa wood, reeds and bamboo lashed together

Rafting becomes less fun in the jungle when there are crocodiles, but deep down I still love it!

Today simple rafts are still a means of transport and trading around the world.

Paul, our soundman, and me on a raft minutes before we were circled by a tiger shark.

with vine, but more modern designs use sealed chambers of air, including barrels and drums, or man-made materials including rubber and polystyrene blocks.

REED RAFTS

Rafts made from reed bundles were used as long as 6000 years ago by the Ancient Egyptians and are still used today by the Uros tribe on Lake Titicaca in South America who live on floating islands made of totora, a type of giant bulrush. Virtually unsinkable, reed rafts are perfect for creating huge platforms capable of carrying both humans and livestock.

BALSA RAFTS

I have made rafts out of balsa in the jungles of Central America. Balsa is a great wood for rafts as it floats very well but is very light to move around, to cut and to work with. The bark from the balsa tree peels off easily in strips and makes very strong lashings. To build a balsa raft, I tend to use around six neck-thick trunks about 3 metres in length laid side by side. Then I find two thinner trunks and lay them at 90 degrees to the thicker trunks, one at each end. I lash the main structure to these two cross-struts using the bark of the trunk as rope.

BAMBOO RAFTS

Bamboo's combination of flexibility, strength and hollowness makes for another excellent raft building material. In fact many communities still use bamboo for high-rise scaffolding in cities as it is so strong and flexible and grows huge! The building technique for rafts is simple. Select good size bamboos and cut them down, then chop them at a height before they start to thin too much towards the top. Drill holes through each individual bamboo at both ends and in the middle and then push through either a length of thinner bamboo or some green wood and lash the structure together. You will need at least two layers of thick bamboo to be confident the raft is sturdy enough.

CORACLES

Coracles were first recorded by Julius Caesar but have been in use in Britain since well before the time of the Romans. Usually in the form of a simple oval construction with a flat bottom, they were traditionally made of interwoven willow tied together with willow bark. The outer layer was then made of animal skin waterproofed with tar, with the finished craft floating on the water like a cork.

Brilliant! A coracle still in use in the UK today.

Due to their shallow draught, coracles are particularly suited to shallow, rocky rivers and were traditionally used for salmon fishing, with two men in separate coracles holding a net between them. Similar craft, called gufas, were used in Iraq, as were skin-covered coracles, called parisals, in India and Tibet. The American Indians also used similar craft, which were called bull-boats. Larger versions up to 2 metres in diameter are still used as river ferries in some parts of India, and are seen on the rivers Teifi and Tywi in Wales. (I even have a friend who floats regularly down the Thames past the barge on which he used to live to go for a drink at the local pub! Brilliant.)

BUILDING A RAFT

A raft is basically anything that floats and will safely carry you and your mates down a river or out into the middle of a lake. For the purist, the best type of raft is one that uses found natural materials like the branches of trees or logs, and you should design your raft to suit whatever materials are available.

Putting the finishing touches to my desert-island raft in Indonesia.

In truth most rafts that you see being paddled down a river in a raft race will be made of a mix of materials including styrofoam, plastic barrels or tin drums strapped together to form a pontoon under a deck of planks or plywood. The advantage of using plastic barrels as a buoyancy device (assuming they are tough and watertight) is that they are much lighter than wood and can easily be carried by two or more of the raft's crew. And while longer, thinner rafts will move much quicker through the water, a square raft that sits on a pontoon above the surface will be much more stable as long as it isn't over-buoyant and too high above the waterline.

LOG RAFTS

Find around half-a-dozen logs at least 10 centimetres in diameter and about 1.5 metres long. The straighter and more uniform they are the better. Place them side-by-side on the ground. Then lay across them, down the whole length of the structure, as many branches (bamboo is preferable if you can find it) as you can find. The branches form the deck and should be about 3 centimetres in diameter and about a metre long. Their width will dictate the final width of the raft. Nail or lash with rope the branches to the logs.

Buoyancy is always the key problem to be solved with home-made rafts, but the wider (and higher, in terms of decking) the raft is, the more buoyant it will be. In the absence of natural materials, watertight plastic bottles, containers or sheets of styrofoam are a good substitute. Turn the raft over and firmly lodge these in the cavities between the logs sealing them in place with sheets of canvas or sacking nailed to the logs.

Steering a raft is also difficult and while a sail can be rigged, it is easier (and usually more effective) to rig an A-frame tiller. You can make one by lashing together narrow poles and fixing them between the branches of the deck as a support for a longer pole at right angles that can be used as a rudder. (Attach the two upright supports vertically, then squeeze them together and lash into an inverted V. Into the top of the V lash the long rudder pole.)

PONTOON RAFTS

This is one of the simplest and most effective raft designs. Find three wooden poles about 3 metres long and no more than about 10 centimetres in diameter, and another four poles about 2 metres long.

Lay the four shorter poles on the ground so that they are all parallel. Now make the gap between the inner poles double that of between

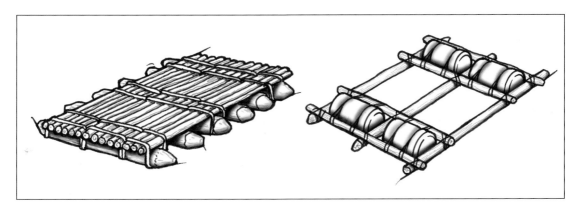

the outer poles. Lay the three longer poles at 90 degrees and at equal intervals over the shorter poles and lash together with rope to produce a platform grid that forms the deck.

Turn over and strap four large watertight plastic barrels between the outer poles. The raft can then be safely paddled by four occupants seated in the four outer spaces of the grid above the plastic containers.

CORACLES

Coracles, a bit like a circular basin made of branches, can easily be constructed using branches of hazel or willow which should be laid out on the ground in a grid formation and then lashed together at their crossing points with string. The structure then needs to be tensioned into its basin shape by pulling up the branches at opposite ends and temporarily tying them together like bowstrings across the middle of the bowl.

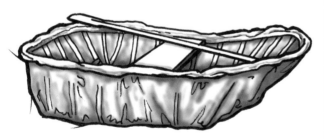

The rim should then be threaded together with other flexible pieces of vine or willow so that the coracle holds its shape. Although animal skins would traditionally have been used to cover the bottom of the boat, a plastic sheet or tarpaulin will do just as well.

Sailing a coracle is an art in itself as paddling to one side causes it to go round in circles. The correct technique uses a figure-of-eight sculling motion.

River races are big team sports nowadays and a great way to see a country and challenge yourself.

Coracle regattas are held every year on the River Severn at Ironbridge and at Leintwardine in Shropshire in the UK.

RAFT RACES

Charity raft races are held every year on Britain's rivers, with prizes handed out for the most imaginative craft, the fancy dress of their

occupants . . . and also for crossing the finishing line first, although, it has to be said, not everyone makes it.

The biggest and the best is the hundred-mile raft race along the River Wye in Herefordshire over the spring Bank Holiday in May. The race has been going for thirty years, starting in Hay-on-Wye and finishing in Chepstow, with the fastest rafts covering the course in around ten and a half hours.

The biggest and the best is the hundred-mile raft race along the River Wye, with the fastest rafts covering the course in about 10½ hours.

Kon-Tiki in full sail – my favourite raft adventure story.

FAMOUS RAFTS

THE *KON-TIKI* EXPEDITION

In 1947 the Norwegian explorer Thor Heyerdahl made an historic 4300-mile crossing of the Pacific Ocean from South America to Polynesia aboard his raft *Kon-Tiki*. Heyerdahl believed that Indians from South America colonized the Polynesian islands but none of the scientific establishments of the day would take him seriously. The expedition was mounted to prove that it was possible.

The raft, named after a Peruvian sun god, was made only from natural materials and using only craft skills that would have been available to the indigenous inhabitants of South America before the arrival of Columbus. These included using balsa tree trunks for the main platform covered in split bamboo for a deck, ropes made of hemp, pine for a stabilizing centreboard, an A-frame mast and a steering oar made of mangrove. The design was based on drawings of Indian rafts made by the first conquistadors.

Heyerdahl and his five-man crew set sail from Peru's Callao Harbour on 28 April 1947, and although they were equipped with some modern equipment (radio, watches, charts, sextant and metal knives), they had no life-saving equipment and nothing that would make the raft itself easier to sail than the original craft. The crew carried 250 litres of water in bamboo tubes along with coconuts and sweet potatoes, but otherwise their diet was the fish they caught which included yellow fin tuna, bonito, flying fish and shark.

The raft was not easy to steer and was propelled only by the winds and the current. But after 101 days at sea, the *Kon-Tiki* made landfall on a coral reef near the uninhabited Polynesian island of Raroia.

Thor resisted the modern advice to use wire to hold the balsa together and the crew soon realized that, over time, wire would have cut through the balsa, whereas the hemp gave some vital 'give' to the structure. They also discovered that as the raft collected algae on the hull the long trail and weight of this actually added stability to the craft in the big storms and swells. The lesson, in short, was that the Indians got it right long before we deemed to believe such a feat was possible!

FIRST MARINERS PROJECT

The First Mariners project was launched in 1996 to investigate the origins of seafaring using rafts that replicate those of the original seafarers. As a result of archaeological finds on the island of Bali in Indonesia, it is now thought possible that the first sea crossings were made as long ago as 850,000 years.

The first full-scale, seagoing bamboo raft was launched in February 1998 and the Timor Sea was crossed on the *Nale Tasih 2* in December 1998, replicating the first landfall in Australia perhaps 60,000 years ago. In October 1999, the project was extended to the Mediterranean region and in January 2000, a primitive raft with 14 men, the *Nale Tasih 4*, repeated the first known sea crossing between Bali and Lombok, Indonesia.

HUCK FINN AND TOM SAWYER

The heroes of one of the most famous adventure stories of all time, Mark Twain's *Huckleberry Finn*, sailed on a raft a thousand miles down the Mississippi River. In the story Huck tries to escape from a drunken father and falls in with Jim, a black runaway slave, who he tries to help escape.

In recognition of the iconic power of the book on the American imagination and its significance as a metaphor for self-resilience, the values of the original pioneers and the American way of life, Tom Sawyer Island was one of the original attractions when Disneyland opened in 1956 with visitors being ferried to the island by raft. In my eyes the book deserves every ounce of its success. It is a brilliant reminder that life requires us to 'paddle our own canoe', to live boldly, overcome prejudice and hardships and to learn from nature if we are to succeed in the game of life.

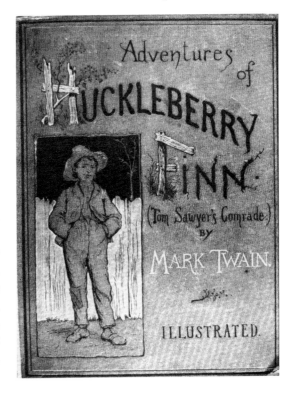

Rock and Sea Cliff Climbing

Life on the Edge

16

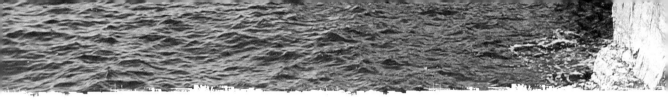

It was hard not to fall in love with Shara!

I CONSIDER ROCK CLIMBING, and sea cliff climbing high above the swell, about as pure a form of self-expression as it's possible to find. And the more I do it, the more I love it! Yet, the more I climb with other people, the more I realize how many crazily talented climbers there are and how much better many of them are than me!

But the magic of climbing is that at heart it requires a spirit of 'togetherness' rather than of competition. Trying to out-do a friend can be so shallow, but climbing together with a good buddy, helping each other, sharing moments of weakness, nerves and achievement, is bonding, intimate and strengthening. That's the real reason I climb. To me it is not about the adrenalin, or fear, it's about sharing moments of struggle, where life becomes raw and is reduced to what really matters. Climb with someone and you learn more about them as a person in one hour than in a week of normal life. I like that.

Exposure to height makes us all vulnerable, but if we can share that vulnerability with each other we create bonds, and where there are bonds there is also strength. That's why so few rock faces on earth can claim to be truly unclimbable. When humans work together for a shared dream, there are few challenges that cannot be met. It is this spirit of exploration and endeavour deep within us all that I thrive on.

So often that spirit within us gets buried underneath the fluff of life, whether it's status, possessions, jobs or money. But I believe that all such things leave us empty, and it is not until we can shake off those ties and allow ourselves to breathe and strive and listen to that voice within that says 'why not?' instead of 'why?' that we come alive.

Climbing on rock is all about poise and balance, not about brute strength. I have seen rock faces reduce the biggest, most macho hulks to gibbering wrecks, while on other occasions they can elevate a quiet, nervous, sensitive soul into a serious rock-jock! Like Selection for the Special Forces, rock climbing puts us under real pressure and, like a grape when it's squeezed, it then shows us what we are really made of inside.

Rock climbing is all about understanding the rock, looking for the smallest line of weakness hidden among the sheer vertiginous cliff in front of you. It is this line of weakness that will show you a way up the face. When you find it and overcome it and roll over the edge onto the top, heaving for breath, that moment is hard to beat. Why? Because in achieving that goal we are fulfilling our potential.

And being good at climbing requires the same dedication as being good at living. To fulfil our capabilities in life we need to exercise, eat well and keep healthy. Likewise with a climb, it is all about good preparation. Good climbers build up to the big moments through long hours of hard training and dedication . . . and the rock rewards them in return. This is how climbers are able to scale hundreds and hundreds of metres of seemingly impenetrable rock walls.

I have had the great privilege of rock climbing all around the world, from the wadis of the Sahara and Oman to the sheer gems of Copper Canyon in Mexico and the 'Lion King' Pride

Exposure to height makes us all vulnerable, but if we can share that vulnerability with each other we create bonds, and where there are bonds there is also strength.

Me wadi climbing in Oman.

Sea-cliff climbing on my favourite route on our island in North Wales.

Rock in Kenya. But my favourite climb is in North Wales, up a small rock face leading up from the sea to the top of the cliff where we have a small home, hidden away, all on its own. The climb itself takes me to my limit, but I remember climbing that face for the first time, sitting on the top recovering, looking across at the blue sea and then down below to the white surf, with my wife and children nearby in the house – it was pure heaven. It's in that sort of moment that I know why I truly love to climb sea cliffs and rock faces. Life becomes reduced to the simple, the satisfying and to that tingling in your bones of quiet achievement against the odds of gravity.

My wife Shara couldn't understand why the first thing I did when we bought this tumbledown wreck of a cottage above a wild sea cliff was to put in anchor points on the cliff. 'Surely some windows and a basin take priority over these, don't they?'

I sighed. Some things are impossible to explain!

Climbing together is all about trust and communication.

THE HISTORY OF ROCK CLIMBING

Man has always had the instinct to climb. In part this may be down to our tree-climbing ancestors and the need to explore and survive in an ever-changing world. Whatever the reason, the history of rock climbing stretches back into prehistory. There are many cliff dwellings and tombs around the world that would have required what we think of today as technical climbing skills to ascend and descend.

Modern rock climbing evolved from the Victorian passion for Alpine mountain climbing. Many of the most challenging mountainous areas in the British Isles were deliberately sought out and used as training grounds for the rigours of the Alpine peaks. In the process a new sport was born, and instead of focusing entirely on the goal of reaching the summit by whatever means, the climber's goal was to test himself against the most challenging routes and rock faces.

In the UK, the sport of climbing for the sheer thrill of conquering a seemingly unclimbable rock face can be traced back to Walter Haskett who made the first solo ascent of Napes Needle in the Lake District in 1886. In the early decades of the

In the early days, only the most basic climbing aids were available – mostly in the form of a tweed jacket, a flask of coffee and a short length of rope.

Me at the start of a sea cliff climb in the South Pacific.

twentieth century, rock climbing began to gain momentum in the US and throughout Europe, particularly in Germany.

In the early days, only the most basic climbing aids were available – mostly in the form of a tweed jacket, a flask of coffee and a short length of rope. But as time went by and artificial aids were developed in the form of pitons and chockstones, a debate began as to the relative merits of 'free climbing' and 'aid climbing'.

It's a debate that continues to this day. The former is when a climber depends solely on their body strength and skill to climb a rock face and uses ropes and other climbing equipment only to prevent serious injury in the event of a fall. Aid climbers, on the other hand, use both the equipment they have on them and other available aids like bolts drilled into the rock face to pull themselves up or to stand on as they climb. Although some of the world's toughest climbs are only possible as aided climbs, the spirit of the modern sport is very much in the free climbing camp.

CLIMBING STYLES

Depending on the terrain, the type of rock, its difficulty and the experience of the climbers involved, over the years a wide variety of climbing styles have evolved.

LEAD CLIMBING

This is the traditional method of climbing, where an experienced climber ascends a rock face putting in place a series of removable anchor points as he goes. Although he is attached to a safety rope being fed out by a belayer who remains on the ground, until he puts an anchor point in place he may seriously injure himself if he falls. The rest of the climbing group, who will normally be less experienced, follow the lead climber's route up the rock face 'clipping in' to the anchor points as they go so that they will be held in the event of a fall. The last climber up removes the anchor points from the rock face as he climbs.

Big wall climbing needs courage, power and reliable gear!

TOP ROPING

Top roping is safer than lead climbing as from the start a rope is attached to an anchor that has been placed at the top of a cliff or rock face before the climb begins. The lead climber is attached to one end of a rope that runs up the cliff, through the anchor at the top and back down again to a belayer at the foot of the face. In the event of a fall (and assuming the belayer is paying attention), the climber will fall a minimal distance before he is held.

Top roping has the advantage of a low environmental impact and allows climbers to safely attempt the most challenging routes. The only drawback for some is that the route up is necessarily restricted to the area of the rock face directly underneath the anchor and does not allow the flexibility of exploring other more circuitous routes.

SPORT CLIMBING

The emphasis in sport climbing, a form of aided climbing, is on the athletic prowess of the climber on often extremely challenging wall climbs with pre-placed permanent anchors in the rock face. This method of climbing eliminates the need for carrying cumbersome gear – the only equipment required is a rope and some quickdraws (see below). Armed with this, all the climber has to do is attach one end of the 'draw' to the fixed bolt on the rock face and the other to his climbing rope, leaving him free to focus on the technical aspects of the ascent.

BOULDERING

The new kid on the block in the climbing world, bouldering focuses on seemingly impossible sequences up short sections of rock or boulders. The emphasis is not just on height and

Part of the magic of climbing is focus, peace and togetherness.

Bouldering: the ultimate training ground.

DEEP WATER SOLOING

Free solo climbing over water (lake or sea) allows the climber to climb unencumbered by gear with the knowledge that a fall will be into water, and not onto hard, unforgiving rock. This method of climbing became very popular in the 1980s at locations such as Lulworth Cove in Dorset. But be careful how high you go unroped. Hitting water at an awkward angle (i.e. during a fall) from a great height can be like hitting concrete!

TECHNIQUES/EQUIPMENT/JARGON

Rock climbing, like most adventure sports, has its fair share of specialist techniques, equipment and jargon. These are just a few of the most common bits of kit you will come across in your climbing career.

BELAYS AND BELAY DEVICES

A belay is the most widely used safety technique in climbing. A belay is a form of 'protection' where a rope is attached to the climber, runs up

inaccessibility but also on sheer difficulty – the smaller the handholds or the steeper the overhang the better. Instead of ropes and anchors, boulderers use mats to protect themselves in the event of a fall. Bouldering is also an indoor sport with its own international competition circuit.

SOLO AND FREE SOLO CLIMBING

The term 'solo climbing' is usually used to describe climbers who climb alone but carry safety measures in the form of ropes and a self-belay system. It is often confused with free solo climbing – the ultimate form of purist climbing but also the most dangerous – where the climber takes on a rock face without any protective equipment whatsoever.

A belayer: his partner's life is in his hands.

And it takes balls (although some of the best free climbers are actually women).

The term 'solo climbing' is usually used to describe climbers who climb alone but carry safety measures in the form of ropes and a self-belay system.

the face and through an anchor at the top of the pitch, and then down again to the 'belayer'. As the climber ascends, the belayer takes up the slack length of rope to ensure that the climber will not drop far if they lose their footing on the rock face. The belayer can hold the entire weight of his fellow climber with relatively little effort even if the climber is considerably heavier and has actually fallen from the rock face. Climbers take it in turns to be 'on belay' during an ascent.

A belay device is attached to the belayer's harness and acts as a friction brake on a climbing rope ensuring that the fall of a climber can be brought to a rapid but not instant halt.

PITCH AND MULTI-PITCHES

A pitch is a section of a climb that requires only one rope length between two belay points. Multi-pitch climbing is the ascent of climbing routes with one or more stops at a belay station. The leader ascends the pitch anchoring himself to the belay station as he goes, before the other climbers in the team follow behind.

CARABINERS, NUTS, QUICKDRAWS AND SLINGS

CARABINERS
A weight-bearing metal loop, often in a D-shape and usually made from aluminium alloy, that has a finger-screw or spring-loaded opening gate in one side. They are mostly used for attaching rope to fixed anchors.

NUTS
These are the small blocks of tapered or hexagonal metal you will see hanging on lengths of looped wire from climber's harnesses. They are used for wedging into small cracks in a rock face as a safety device that will lock into the rock face in the event of a fall.

QUICKDRAWS
Often known as 'draws', these devices consist of two non-locking carabiners attached by a sling and are used in aided climbing to attach ropes to bolts in the rock face.

SLINGS
Loops of webbing that can be attached to other pieces of equipment or anchors to provide an extension or reach around an anchor point.

ANCHORS AND RUNNERS
Points in the rock face where carabiners, nuts and ropes connected to a climber are attached as safety devices so the climber will be held in the event of a fall.

ABSEILING/RAPPELLING
The English and American words respectively for the technique of descending a rock face using ropes and a friction device to control speed.

CLIMBING GRADES

Rock climbing as a sport grew in popularity in different countries at different times and grading systems were developed which categorized known climbing routes according to difficulty. In this way a new climber would know what they were up against, its relative difficulty compared to other routes, and the likelihood of their being able to climb it successfully. But the result was that different grading systems are now used in different countries.

These vary from the UK adjectival grades (Moderate, Difficult, Very Difficult, etc.) to the numerical technical grades used in the US and the rest of Europe. If you really want to grapple with the relative merits of an Alpine V11+ and a US 5.11b, try looking up mountaindays.net. In the meantime you'd do best just to enjoy the thrill of a rock face and not get too bogged down in classifications!

SEA CLIFF AND SEA STACK CLIMBING

The cliffs of West Penwith in Cornwall around Land's End are the home of sea cliff climbing. It was here that in 1902 A. W. Andrews first put into practice the inspired idea of combining the joys of rock climbing with the sheer pleasure of being beside (all right then, dangling high above) the sea.

I'm not sure whether it's the reward of a snooze and a good view at the top or the sheer variety of rocks and routes for everyone from novices to rock jocks that makes the sport so compelling. But the 'granite kingdom' is still at the heart of the sea cliff climbing scene. The sport has now become popular all over the UK and Anglesey, Pembrokeshire and north-west Scotland in particular have some truly awe-inspiring cliff climbs.

But for many sea cliff enthusiasts, the literally hundreds of sea stacks scattered around the coast of the UK are the 'holy grail' of sea climbing. Sea stacks are those massive towers of rock that seem to spring out of the sea just off the coast like the outlying defenders of the land against the pounding sea.

Climbing requires focus and concentration at all times.

Sea stacks are often associated with legends of wandering giants turned to stone and it's not hard to see why. They are in fact the eroded remains of the cliff face before its more porous surroundings were washed away over time by the merciless attentions of sea, wind and tide, leaving lonely towers of rock isolated from the land. There are more than 250 of them alone off the coast of Scotland but the most famous trio of all lie off the coast of Orkney – the Old Man of Hoy, the Old Man of Stoer and Am Buachaille at Sandwood Bay. Each has become a climbing legend in its own right.

THE OLD MAN OF HOY

Located off the coast of Orkney adjacent to some of the highest sea cliffs in the UK, the Old Man of Hoy was made famous in 1967 by Chris Bonington and his team who made a live BBC outside broadcast watched by millions when the team repeated their successful first summit attempt of the previous year.

At 130 metres high, it is made of decaying red sandstone and is thought have been joined body and soul to the mainland as recently as 400 years ago. An arch connecting it to the mainland collapsed in the 1950s and the Old Man himself is predicted to sink into the sea some time later this century.

Nevertheless as many as fifty ascents of the Old Man of Hoy are made every year and a record of each climb is kept in an RAF logbook in a Tupperware container safely buried in a small cairn on the summit.

Sea stacks – one of the most exhilarating forms of climbing around.

ROCK GODS AND GODDESSES

CHRIS SHARMA

For the last decade, Californian Chris Sharma (born 1981) has carved out a reputation as the best and most famous climber in the world today. He started out climbing trees in his back yard from the tender age of five and by the time he was in his early teens had already clocked a number of high profile first ascents and competition successes, becoming a professional rock climber at sixteen.

His most famous climbs include a first ascent of the world famous sport route Realization in Céüse, France, which he completed in July 2001, and is considered by many to be the first successful 8b/5.15a/9a+ climb (i.e. well off the top of the scale of all the different grading systems!).

Sharma talks about his 'intimate relationship with the rock' and has a spiritual and meditative approach to his climbing, taking on routes that require a combination of strength, creative technique and precise movement. A keen exponent of bouldering, he has most recently taken up deep-water soloing without ropes or harnesses with only the safety of a fall into the water below for protection.

LYNN HILL AND KATIE BROWN

Lynn Hill (born 1961) began her climbing career at the age of fourteen, learning basic techniques from her sister in California's Joshua Tree National Park, before graduating to more serious rock walls in Yosemite with her then boyfriend, the well-known climber John Long.

In the 1980s she carved out an international reputation as one of the world's top women climbers, winning more than thirty international competitions. She is perhaps most famous for

Woman and mountain in harmony.

being the first person, either male or female, to free climb the Nose, a famous route on El Capitan, a 915-metre vertical rock wall in Yosemite Valley. The next year (1994) she topped the feat by becoming the first person to free climb the route in twenty-four hours.

Katie Brown (born 1980) earned her reputation as the world's best female sport climber by winning numerous international competitions including the World Cup and the ARCO Invitational when she was just a teenager. One of her most famous climbs was an 'on sight' ascent of Omaha Beach in the Red River Gorge in Kentucky in 1999.

Latterly Katie has given up competitive sport climbing to concentrate on traditional climbing. Recent climbing feats include an ascent of the Leaning Tower in Yosemite Valley with Lynn Hill and deep-water soloing with no protective equipment on the cliffs in Malta.

Mountain Climbing

The Ultimate Challenge

Mountains have the ability to test us like no other challenge can.

IT'S STRANGE TO THINK that for centuries mountains were regarded as forbidding, evil places that were to be feared and avoided. Not only were they considered dangerous and unpredictable, but their wild, untamed nature also went against early civilization's thirst for control and uniformity. Pioneering travellers through the Alps would by custom turn their heads away from the mountains, shielding their eyes from those monsters of chaos and their hidden, inexplicable powers.

It was only when people began to conquer their natural fear of the unknown and venture further into the mountains that they began to appreciate them for what they really are. Today, these same mountains are rightly regarded as places of great strength, beauty, wonderment and God-filled power. Man's quest for knowledge and experience, coupled with a very natural desire for freedom and expression, has opened a whole new world to those who are bold enough to step into their shadows.

The freedom, expression and simple wonderment found in mountains is something that has touched my life many times. It has also led me to risk my life at times in pursuit of a

was hooked on the feelings that flooded through me at that moment. I found it hard to deny that a creator's hand must have somehow been involved. Can mere geology create such beauty?

I remember being humbled by the sheer size of those distant, giant Himalayan peaks that seemed to make all the other mountains I had ever seen seem like toys. I have learnt in life that things that stir your insides with such feelings are good things to follow. Mountains do that for me in spades.

But for me the panorama is only half of the appeal of mountains. The other half is in the actual climbing of them. One of my favourite quotes is from William Blake who wrote:

Great things are done when men and
mountains meet;
This is not done by jostling in the street.

These words explain it all really. Modern life can often seem like one big jostle, a perpetual fluffing up of our feathers, a preening of fancy nothingness. For me this is wholly unsatisfying, it is selling ourselves short of all that life has to offer. In contrast, the 'great things' that Blake writes about are the things that happen deep inside us when we are faced with real challenges. It is these raw, intimate, personal moments that really contain the meaning of our lives. Climbing Mount Everest taught me that. It also taught me that mountains sometimes extract a great price. In the most extreme cases that price can be human

summit; and it is what continues to move me still today. The more I experience mountains, the harder it is to deny they have some sort of soul, something that is almost tangible to those who are quiet enough to hear their heartbeat.

I will never forget my first real taste of mountain grandeur. It was at sunrise in the hills above Darjeeling in Northern India. I was eighteen years old. As the red dawn brushed steadily across the great Himalayan peaks in front of me, like an artist bathing a watercolour in pink wash, I was astonished by what I saw and felt – the smell, the clarity, the overwhelming exhilaration of scale – I

The freedom, expression and simple wonderment found in mountains is something that has touched my life many times.

Constantly changing with the seasons, always intoxicating, always in charge.

life. During our expedition four climbers lost their lives on Everest, and in its unchanging nature the mountain continues its ruthless human culling.

Despite the risks involved with high peaks, men and women risk their lives every day in pursuit of the profound. What it is and why they do it is hard to explain, but I can give a few indications. Reaching the summit of a peak, or just being on a peak for any length of time, requires us to slow down and get our hearts to beat in tune with the mountain. In doing so we are re-finding that natural strength within us that allows us to tackle those peaks, against overwhelming odds; to put ourselves, willingly, unencumbered, wholeheartedly inside the lion's mouth. On the mountains we are the Davids and the peaks are the Goliaths. King David needed great heart to overcome Goliath against such odds; mountains bring out that heart in us. That's why I really love them.

Do you want life to be raw or fluffy? You choose. But if you want to taste life in the raw, then climb some mountains. It puts you back in touch with the real you, the best of you. It is not about conquering or bagging peaks. If we restrict mountain climbing to those shallow pursuits, we miss the point. Mountaineering does not so much build character as reveal it. It is the mountain that dictates a ruthless examination of anyone brave or foolhardy enough to take them on. There are few other activities where you have to put so much trust in yourself and in others.

Mountains cannot be conquered or tamed. The real conquest is in overcoming the fears inside us. Mountain climbing can inspire great courage, humility and strength in men and women (I have witnessed these things many times); and that is what gives mountains their true appeal for me.

'Hang on, I'm sure the path's around here somewhere . . .'

BECAUSE IT'S THERE

One of the most famous quotes ever is the reply the legendary Everest climber George Leigh Mallory gave in 1923 to a reporter on *The New York Times* who asked why he wanted to climb Mount Everest. 'Because it's there,' he said and the phrase passed into legend.

Much less often quoted, however, are Mallory's more considered comments on the same question written the previous year. They shed much light on the question of what motivates men to risk all to stand on top of the world's highest mountains, and reveal the deeper meaning of his more famous quote as well as the philosophy of one of climbing's greatest heroes:

The first question which you will ask and which I must try to answer is this, 'What is the use of climbing Mount Everest?' and my answer must at once be, 'It is no use. There is not the slightest prospect of any gain whatsoever. We shall not bring back a single bit of gold or silver, not a gem, nor any coal or iron. We shall not find a single foot of earth that can be planted with crops to raise food. It's no use.'

So, if you cannot understand that there is something in man which responds to the challenge of this mountain and goes out to meet it, that the struggle is the struggle of life itself, upward and forever upward, then you won't see why we go. What we get from this adventure is just sheer joy. And joy is, after all, the end of life. We do not live to eat and make money. We eat and make money to be able to enjoy life. That is what life means and what life is for.

MAGIC MOUNTAINS

EVEREST

Mount Everest lies on the border of Nepal and Tibet. It's the highest peak in the Himalayas, the greatest range of mountains on earth. For centuries it was known as Chomolungma, or 'Mother of the Universe', by the local Sherpa people, but was dubbed Mount Everest in 1865 by the British in honour of Sir George Everest who first surveyed the region in the 1830s.

Its height is officially put at 29,035 feet or 8848 metres although the mountain is thought to be growing by around 4 millimetres a year due to the

A view across to Makalu taken by Neil and myself from Everest's summit at dawn.

Crevasse crossing on an icefall at 5500 metres on Everest.

Adds a new dimension to a camping trip!

One of my only two photos from the summit of Everest.

A photo I'm pretty proud of – Neil Laughton and me on the summit of Everest planting the SAS regimental flag.

relentless pressure of tectonic plates in the earth's mantle which have been pushing the Himalayas steadily higher for the last sixty million years.

Climbing the world's highest mountain has long been a metaphor for overcoming apparently impossible odds. And in the decades before it was finally summited in 1954 by the New Zealander Edmund Hillary and Sherpa Tenzing Norgay, it earned its reputation by taking the lives of many mountaineers.

The most famous of those early attempts to climb the mountain was made by George Mallory and Andrew 'Sandy' Irvine in 1924, the last of three unsuccessful British expeditions made in the 1920s. The climbers were last seen high on the north-east ridge, within a few hundred metres of the summit, on 8 June by one of the expedition members, Noel Odell. But they were never to be seen again.

Ever since that day, speculation has continued as to whether one or both of the climbers made the summit or were killed before they could reach it. In 1999, the sensational discovery of Mallory's body on the north face reignited the debate. The team also found an altimeter, a pocketknife, monogrammed handkerchiefs, personal letters, goggles and even an unpaid bill on Mallory's body. But the fact that a photograph of his wife that he was intending to leave on the summit was not there appeared to suggest that he might indeed have been successful.

However, the Kodak camera which he was carrying that day – and which may still contain frozen film with photographs that some experts think may be retrievable – has still not been found. The argument that the clothes the climbers wore would not have given them the protection they needed to reach the summit has recently been proven false. Replica climbing clothes painstakingly recreated from the original fibres and made of gabardine, wool, cotton and silk were shown to be highly effective at providing warmth, flexibility and wicking away moisture at high altitude.

The mystery of Mallory continues.

Everest still claims around one in ten lives of those who reach the summit. Technology, equipment, weather reporting and clothing improve . . . but the mountain remains the same: ruthless, unforgiving and unbowed.

K2

The world's second highest mountain, K2, on the border between Pakistan and China in the Karakoram range, is considered one of the hardest and most dangerous mountains in the world to climb. It has earned the nickname the 'Savage Mountain' for the high death rate of those attempting to climb it and its volatile weather. Fewer than 300 climbers have reached the summit of K2, compared with more than 2600 who have climbed Everest.

The factors that make K2 such an overwhelming challenge are its tendency to attract ferocious storms and the steepness and exposure of the routes to the summit. All these problems are magnified by the thinness of the air, which, as on Mount Everest, is around a third of the density found at sea level.

One of the most heroic acts in the history of mountaineering took place on K2 on 10 August 1953 when an American expedition which had been caught in a severe storm at high altitude were trying to descend with a critically ill member of the party. During a traverse at 7500 metres, one of the climbers slipped, pulling five more climbers off the mountain until they were dangling hundreds of feet above the glacier below. If it hadn't been for the strength and decisive action of Pete 'The Belay' Schoening, who managed to brace the rope around his hip, jam a wooden ice axe into the ground behind a boulder and arrest their fall, all but one of the party would have been swept to certain death. The full story of the expedition, a mountaineering classic, is told in *K2 – The Savage Mountain* by Charles Houston and Robert Bates.

Mountains have a way of reminding us what's important.

The Eiger – one of the world's most dangerous climbs, due to the objective dangers of rock falls and avalanches.

THE EIGER AND THE MATTERHORN

Few climbing challenges still inspire as much respect and fear as the infamous north face of the Eiger towering two thousand metres above the Bernese Oberland in the Swiss Alps. Many climbers have died attempting this unforgiving climb, due in part to the severe risk of rockfall and avalanche, as well as its steepness and exposure to the weather.

After climbing the north face at the age of 62, even the normally unflappable British explorer and adventurer Sir Ranulph Fiennes admitted he had found the experience very scary. 'I've been an explorer for more than 25 years, but this was my challenge of a lifetime,' he said. 'I thought it was going to be just a more difficult version of the practice climbs I have been doing around Chamonix and the Alps. Not the nightmarish thing that it actually was.'

With one of the most distinctive shapes of any mountain in the world (and a replica in Disneyland to boot), the Matterhorn was feared by the early Alpinists who thought it might prove impossible to climb. Located on the Swiss/Italian border, the mountain's four faces are aligned to the cardinal points.

The first attempted climbs to the summit were from the south (Italian) side but these proved harder than expected, and the first route to be climbed to the top was the northern Hörnli route from Zermatt on the Swiss side, in 1865. This is still the most popular route and is climbed by hundreds of people every year.

THE SEVEN SUMMITS

Since the 1980s, when the American Richard Bass climbed them all, the feat of standing on the peak of the highest mountain on each continent has been one of the great mountaineering challenges. Here they are, in order of height:

> **ASIA:**
> Everest (Tibet/Nepal, 8848 metres)
> **SOUTH AMERICA:**
> Aconcagua (Argentina, 6962 metres)
> **NORTH AMERICA:**
> McKinley (Alaska, 6194 metres)
> **AFRICA:**
> Kilimanjaro (Tanzania, 5895 metres)
> **EUROPE:**
> Elbrus (Caucasus, Russia, 5642 metres)
> **ANTARCTICA:**
> Vinson (Sentinel Range, 4892 metres)
> **AUSTRALIA:**
> Kosciuszko (New South Wales, 2228 metres)

But records, after all, count for only half the story. Most mountaineers know that climbing the second highest peaks on each continent would in fact be a far harder task. Almost all are harder to climb than their higher neighbours, the most obvious example being K2, which is acknowledged to be a harder technical climb than Everest.

And as with many such lists, the candidates have been disputed. Some argue that Australia's Mount Kosciuszko (a mountain that can be hiked up) should be replaced with the Carstensz Pyramid (4884 metres) on the island of New Guinea in Indonesia. It all comes down to how you define the boundaries of the continents.

These tiny ice pinnacles are formed by extreme high winds blasting ice particles together. They tend to point into the prevailing winds.

EDWARD WHYMPER

Edward Whymper, known during his lifetime as the 'Prince of Mountaineers', was the most famous climber of his day. Born in 1840 and the son of an artist-engraver, Whymper joined his father's firm when he left school and soon became a well-known illustrator in his own right.

It was in his professional capacity as an illustrator of a book for the English Alpine Club that Whymper first visited the French Alps in 1860. During the next few seasons he made several first ascents of Alpine peaks, culminating on 14 July 1865 with a first ascent of the Matterhorn. But, due to a tragic accident, this event was to haunt him for the rest of his life.

Whymper: the Prince of Mountaineers.

During the descent the most inexperienced member of the party slipped and swept three other climbers with him to their deaths after the rope that was holding them snapped. To this day, the reasons for the tragedy are disputed. An inconclusive inquest was held at the time into the causes of the fall with the suggestion that the rope holding the doomed climbers may have been deliberately cut and weakened by one of the guides who survived or even by Whymper himself. The event was one of the most notorious of the Victorian era.

Whymper went on to lead expeditions in Greenland, the Canadian Rockies and South America where he made important early studies into the causes of altitude sickness. But it was the triumph and tragedy on the Matterhorn that defined his life, as this extract from his *Scrambles Amongst the Alps* so poignantly reveals:

There have been joys too great to be described in words, and there have been griefs upon which I have not dared to dwell; and with these in mind I say: climb if you will, but remember that courage and strength are nought without prudence, and that a momentary negligence may destroy the happiness of a lifetime. Do nothing in haste; look well to each step; and from the beginning think what may be the end.

SIR EDMUND HILLARY AND SHERPA TENZING

While some still maintain that Mallory and Irvine reached the summit of Everest, it is beyond doubt that they never made it down. The laurels for this great feat, one of the most famous in the history of exploration, went to the New Zealander Edmund Hillary and Sherpa Tenzing Norgay of Nepal.

The two reached the summit just in time for the coronation of Queen Elizabeth II on 29 May 1953, as part of a British expedition led by John

Hillary and Tenzing, my heroes.

Bonington climbed with legendary mountaineering names including Don Whillans, Dougal Haston, Doug Scott, Peter Boardman and Joe Tasker, many of whom later lost their lives on the world's great mountains.

Bonington's ethos was to attempt extreme climbs with the minimum possible equipment while taking greater and greater risks in the pursuit of new first ascents and new, more challenging routes to summits already climbed. Bonington led, or was a member of, nineteen expeditions to the Himalayas, including an ascent of Everest in 1985.

> Bonington's ethos was to attempt extreme climbs with the minimum possible equipment.

Hunt. The pair spent about 15 minutes on the summit and looked briefly for signs of Mallory's 1924 expedition but found nothing. While they were there Sherpa Tenzing buried some food as an offering to the gods of the mountain and Hillary left a crucifix.

Sir Edmund, as he soon became, always maintained that while reaching the summit was a very satisfying moment, his proudest achievement in life was his work for the Himalayan Trust, which he founded to help the Sherpa people of the Khumbu region of Nepal.

SIR CHRIS BONINGTON

A keen rock climber from his early teens, Chris Bonington (born 1934) was the unofficial leader of a group of climbers in the golden era of British Himalayan climbing in the years after the first ascent of Everest.

Sir Chris Bonington (left), one of our greatest climbers.

KNOTS

The art of knots is all about being able to tie a few good all-rounders that will get you out of a scrape when it really matters. If you neglect this simple skill, then when the critical time comes, your fingers will shake, your mind will swirl and the knot will fail. As will the raft, kite or tree house that is depending on it. It only takes a few minutes to learn a knot and once you've used it in action several times, it will sink into your subconscious ready to surface again when it really matters. Practise it again and again until it's second nature. Then you're good to go!

USEFUL JARGON

Describing accurately how to tie a knot can be complicated even if the knot itself, once learned, is relatively easy. Knowing what part of the rope is being referred to, or what action is being described, will make it far easier to learn.

Working End/Part: The end, or section, of the rope that is being used to tie the knot.
Standing End/Part: The end, or section, of the rope that is not being used to tie the knot.
Bight: A bight is when the rope is turned back on itself to form a U. The bight is the middle section of a rope.
Turn: A turn of the rope around another object so that the rope crosses itself.
Loop: A loop in the rope made by passing the working end over itself in the shape of a circle.

TYPES OF KNOT

The following definitions of the main categories of knots use the word 'rope', but this can equally apply to lengths of cord, vine, canvas or any other pieces of material, which need to be tied together.

BENDS

Used for tying the ends of two lengths of rope together. The relative thickness of each end and the type of material they are made of will determine the best bend to use.

HITCHES

A temporary knot used to tie an object that needs to be held in one place, like a boat or a horse, to a fixed object like a bollard or post. Most hitches tighten under load, but may come undone when slack. Can be quickly loosened by untying in reverse.

LOOPS

A loop knot is formed by attaching the working end of a rope to the standing end so that it stays the same size and does not slip. The bowline is the most famous form of loop.

SLIP KNOTS

A slip knot is formed by attaching the working end of a rope to the standing end so that it will, on purpose, tighten under tension.

STOPPERS

This is a simple knot tied in the end of a rope to stop it being pulled back through an opening like a block or a pulley. Stopper knots are also used to weigh a rope down if it is being thrown or as a convenient handhold.

BINDING, LASHING & WHIPPING

There are many other categories of knot. These include binding knots for holding loose packages together, lashing knots for holding different objects together, and whipping knots for stopping frayed ends from unravelling.

BASIC KNOTS

BOWLINE

Type: Loop
Uses: The bowline is one of the most widely used – and useful – knots. If you only learn one knot so you can tie it in your sleep, this is the one! The bowline creates a loop at the end of a rope that will neither slip nor tighten, but which can also be easily adjusted and untied. This is its secret and why it is so often used at sea and in rescue work. Many a drowning sailor or stranded mountaineer has been pulled to safety with a rope tied in a bowline around their waist.
Technique: Take the working end round (or through) the object to which the rope is being attached. Then make a loop in the standing part and push the working end through from below. Next take the working end under the standing part and back through the loop. Pull tight. Best remembered with the old scouting aide-memoire, 'A rabbit comes out of the hole, goes around the tree, and back down the hole.'
Advantages: Reliable under load.
Disadvantages: May loosen and untie if not under load. (So secure with a hitch in the remaining part of the working end.)

KLEMHEIST

Type: Friction hitch
Uses: A 'slide and grip' knot that can be attached to another rope to make foot- or handholds that tighten under tension. Can be moved backwards or forwards when the tension is released. Klemheists have saved many lives in self-rescue situations in mountain and crevasse.

Technique: A klemheist is tied by making turns with a piece of looped cord around another, thicker rope. Wrap the loop round the main rope a minimum of four times. Thread the bottom end of the loop through the top end. Then pull tight, making sure the turns lie neatly and symmetrically side by side.

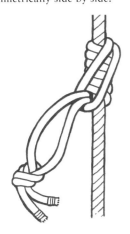

Advantages: Lighter and less bulky than mechanical rope-grabs. Can be moved both up and down by releasing tension. Can be improvised from other equipment like a strip of webbing. (Better than a regular prusik as the klemheist can be released easily after it has been loaded.)

Disadvantages: May not work on rope that is greasy or frozen. The closer in size the looped cord and the rope, the less efficiently the klemheist will work.

FIGURE OF EIGHT

Type: Stopper

Uses: Prevents the end of a rope being pulled free of a pulley system, block or retaining device. Often used at sea to stop the ropes attached to sails (known as sheets) from slipping free. Can also be used on the working end of another knot to stop it working itself undone.

Technique: Make a U-shape (bight) near the working end of the rope and then twist it to form a loop. Then pass the working end round the standing end and back through the loop and pull tight.

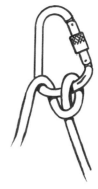

Advantages: Quick and easy to tie and can be easily undone.

Disadvantages: The thicker the rope, the more likely it is to shake loose.

CLOVE HITCH

Type: Hitch

Uses: Lashing a rope to a fixed pole, although it can be used in the bight of a rope as an anchor point.

Technique: Make a turn of the rope round a pole, making sure the working end is on top. Then make a second turn around the pole and pass the working end under the second loop. Pull tight.

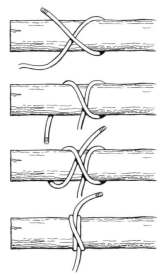

Advantages: Very easy to adjust and untie in situations where the length of the standing end of the rope needs to be varied (mooring a boat alongside a jetty for example).

Disadvantages: Will slip if not pulled tight. Technically a clove hitch is only secure if loaded at each end.

ITALIAN HITCH

Type: A variation on the clove hitch.

Advantages: A good, fast knot to abseil on.

Disadvantages: Be aware on long abseils that the bottom of the rope will twist up on itself.

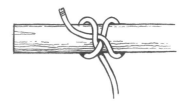

SPAR HITCH

Type: A variation on the clove hitch.

Advantages: More secure than the clove hitch when using wet or synthetic ropes.

SHEETBEND

Type: Bend

Uses: Tying the ends of two pieces of rope together. These can be of equal or differing diameter and the knot will still be effective.

Technique: Take the larger piece of rope in one hand and make a U-bend (bight) in one end, holding it in place with fingers and thumb. Then with the other hand, push the end of the smaller rope through the U from below. Now take it over the working end of the U and back under the standing end before finally tucking the working end of the smaller rope back under itself and pulling the knot tight. If the knot has been tied correctly, the working ends of both ropes will be on the same side.

Advantages: Excellent for tying together ropes of a different size but works fine too if the ropes are the same size.

Disadvantages: Needs two hands to tie and both ropes must be free of any tension or load.

Single

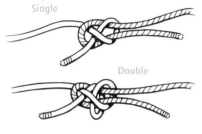

Double

REEF KNOT

Type: Binding knot

Uses: Tying together the ends of two pieces of rope that are the same size to bind a package.

Technique: Take a piece of rope in each hand and place the working end of the rope in your right hand over the working end of the rope in your left hand. Then pass the end of the right hand rope under the other rope and back over (half hitch). Now do the same thing but with the working end of the rope in your left hand over the working end of the rope in your right hand. If the knot has been tied correctly, both of the working ends will be on the same side of the rope. (If they are on opposite sides you have done it wrong and it will be a granny!)

Advantages: Can be easily untied when not under tension.

Disadvantages: Should never be used to tie two ropes together in critical circumstances as the knot can easily fail and is often mistakenly tied as a granny knot.

WHIP KNOT

Type: Lashing

Uses: Tying the fraying ends of a rope to prevent it unravelling further or lashing handles to blades in a survival scenario.

Technique: Lay a short line of cord along the working end of a rope or handle and hold in place with your thumb. Then lash the cord to the rope with several turns of the standing end of the cord until you can remove your thumb. Next make a U-bend (bight) on the vertical line of the cord and continue wrapping the other end around the rope until the vertical end has been completely covered.

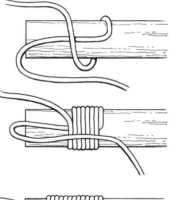

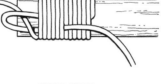

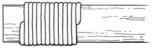

Advantages: Works very effectively if under sufficient tension.

Disadvantages: Can be fiddly to tie and difficult to produce sufficient tension.

LOCKING KNOT

Type: Binding knot

Uses: Very fast and simple and allows you to bind two objects (e.g. logs for a raft) together very tightly.

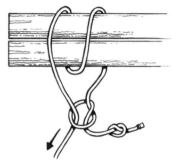

Technique: Take the working end and wrap it twice around the two objects to be tied. Then put a figure of eight into one end and take that same working end and tie it in a simple overhand knot around the other length. Tighten by ratcheting the other length up and down until the two knots meet. Once tight you can add a hitch in the end to ensure it won't slip.

Advantages: Very quick to tie. Secure.

Disadvantages: Once tied tight it can be very hard to untie.

THE ASHLEY BOOK OF KNOTS

First published in 1944 and still in print, this book is a treasure trove of information about the history and uses of almost 4000 knots with more than 7000 drawings and instructions on how to tie them. It has become the standard reference work on the art of tying knots.

CAMOUFLAGE

Camouflage can mean the difference between life and death on combat operations. But when the objective is the pure thrill of outdoor adventuring, it can still have its uses. Learning to merge into the natural world is crucial if you want to observe wild creatures in their natural habitat. And if the objective is to outwit your mates in a paintballing skirmish in the woods, effective camouflage will be even more important!

All the principles that I was taught during Special Forces training were based on the 5 Ss – Shape, Shine, Silhouette, Shadow and Sound.

SHAPE
Break up the very distinctive shape of head and shoulders that distinguishes us as humans.

Good camouflage involves breaking up unnatural shapes and blending in subtly.

SILHOUETTE
Never follow ridge tops where your silhouette can easily be seen against the sky by anyone on lower ground.

SHADOW
Don't let your shadow give you away in bright sunlight or on moonlit nights. Keep in the shadow of trees and undergrowth.

And finally:

SOUND
Keep schtum; breathe softly; and don't sneeze!

Neutral hues, broken lines and stealth.

SHINE
Cover or disguise anything that catches the light and might give you away like glistening silver watches or metal lace eyes. Smear them with mud if necessary.

If you don't believe me, watch and learn from the animals.

To my good friends with whom I love messing about in the great outdoors!

Shara, Jesse & Marmaduke Grylls, Trucker, Alice and Alfie Goodwin-Hudson, Mick, Emma & George Crosthwaite, Neil & Caroline Laughton, Woody & Stani, Gilo, Chloe & Otto Cardozo, Dan Etheridge, Steve Rankin, Scott Tankard, Rupert Smith, Chris Richards, Michael Foster, Hugo, Arabella & Hubie Mackenzie-Smith, Sam & Anna Sykes, Dave Pearce, Nick Parks, Ash Alexander-Cooper, Charlie Mackesy, Lara, James, Mungo, Bevan and Tallulah Fawcett, Charlie Laing, Nige Thompson, Simon, Maddie & Ralph Reay, Mac Mackay, Paul Ritz, Pete Lee, Danny Cane, Duncan Gaudin, Tom & Diana Clowes, Mike Town, Ben Clowes, Mgu Giles, Henry Morley, Charlie V-B, Wogster, Henry Elstub, Chris Hutch, Dom S-B, Shay O'Brian, Adrian Bignell, Nick Smith, Tim Levy, Kevin Smith, Alastair Collins, Paul Morrell, Eric Loth, Jean-Marie Florent, Charlie Bell, Tim and Henny E-C, Ed, Katharine & Emmeline Amies, Jules Slocock, David Hempleman-Adams, Lt-Cdr Al Veale, Andy Leivers, Phill Elston, Annabel, Guy, Benjie, Hamish and Saskia Bignell, Mitty, Watty Hepburne-Scott, Nicky Gumbel, Ted Heywood, Glenn and Derek, the late Chris Thorn, Rupert and Aurelia Stephenson, Will Collis, Rob Cranham, Owi Jones, Col. David Cooper, Damian Cardozo, Bobby Abedeen, Mark Jackson, and Sgt Bob Williams, Sgt Chris C, Maj. Mal Gibson, Seamus, Jamo, Neil L, Matt Dickinson, Giles L-J, Tpr Bobby P, Tpr Martin P, Smudge, Capt. Pete P, Graham C, Davie C, Stevie H, Steve W, Pete I, John Grif, Capt. Bill B & Robina, Armalite from E Squadron.

And, ultimately to my late dad, Mickey, for introducing me to all this adventure. I hope you are looking down, enjoying everything you have set in motion. And, of course, my mum, apologies for causing you so many heart palpitations!

Also by Bear Grylls
Born Survivor

TRANSWORLD PUBLISHERS
61–63 Uxbridge Road, London W5 5SA
A Random House Group Company
www.rbooks.co.uk

First published in Great Britain
in 2008 by Channel 4 Books
a division of Transworld Publishers

Addresses for Random House Group Ltd companies outside the UK can be found at: www.randomhouse.co.uk
The Random House Group Ltd Reg. No. 954009

The Random House Group Limited supports The Forest Stewardship Council (FSC), the leading international forest-certification organization. All our titles that are printed on Greenpeace-approved FSC-certified paper carry the FSC logo. Our paper procurement policy can be found at www.rbooks.co.uk/environment

Typeset in Sabon and Foundry Sans
Designed by Bobby Birchall, Bobby&Co, London
Printed and bound in Great Britain by
Butler Tanner & Dennis Ltd

2 4 6 8 10 9 7 5 3

PICTURE CREDITS